Reducing Uncertainty

Reducing Uncertainty

INTELLIGENCE ANALYSIS
AND NATIONAL SECURITY

Thomas Fingar

Stanford Security Studies

An Imprint of Stanford University Press

Stanford, California

Stanford University Press

Stanford, California

Special discounts for bulk quantities of Stanford Security Studies are available to corporations, professional associations, and other organizations. For details and discount information, contact the special sales department of Stanford University Press. Tel: (650) 736-1782, Fax: (650) 736-1784

Printed in the United States of America on acid-free, archival-quality paper

Library of Congress Cataloging-in-Publication Data

Fingar, Thomas, author.
    Reducing uncertainty : intelligence analysis and national security / Thomas Fingar.
       pages cm
    Includes bibliographical references and index.
    ISBN 978-0-8047-7593-9 (pbk. : alk. paper) —
    ISBN 978-0-8047-7594-6 (pbk. : alk. paper)
    1. Intelligence service—United States. 2. National security—United States.   I. Title.
    JK468.I6F56 2011
    327.1273—dc22

                            2010045291

Typeset by Thompson Type in 10/14 Minion

Dedicated to the Community of Analysts:
Past, Present, and Future

CONTENTS

ACKNOWLEDGMENTS

THIS BOOK IS A HIGHLY PERSONAL and doubtless somewhat idiosyncratic description of the role of intelligence analysis in the making of national security decisions in the U.S. government. It focuses on analysis because that is the aspect of the process that I know best and, more importantly, because intelligence analysts are at the nexus between decision makers and the vast apparatus constructed to reduce uncertainty by providing information and insight tailored to the specific needs of "customers" ranging from the president and Cabinet secretaries to troops in the field, cops on the beat, members of Congress, desk-level officers in Washington and embassies around the world, developers of military equipment and tactics, and myriad others. During my career, I had opportunities to interact directly with many such customers, at many levels. I also had the privilege of working with and for many dedicated and in certain respects extraordinary intelligence professionals. This book presents my take on a complex set of issues, institutions, and expectations, but my views have been shaped by mentors and colleagues as well as my own experiences. This is the place to thank them for their guidance and to absolve them of responsibility for the judgments and shortcomings of my effort to explain what we do to support the national security enterprise.

I learned to be an analyst as a Cornell undergraduate and as a graduate student at Stanford. My principal advisor and mentor at both schools was John W. Lewis. His pioneering work on leadership in China, intellectual curiosity, and passion for teaching gave me the incentive and the tools to tackle tough subjects and eschew superficial conclusions. These lessons were reinforced by other teachers who later became colleagues at Stanford, including Alex Dallin,

Alex George, and Gabriel Almond. I was quite content at Stanford and probably would not have returned to Washington or full-time intelligence analysis had I not been persuaded to head INR's China Division by Assistant Secretary Mort Abramowitz. He mousetrapped me into a two-year commitment by saying that if I thought I could do better than the performance I had criticized, I should put my career where my mouth was. I did, and have thanked Mort many times for his confidence and for giving me the opportunity.

Mort did not just give me a job, he also, and more importantly, taught me the importance of tailoring analytic support to the concerns, needs, and decision timelines of our national security customers. These lessons were reinforced by two other INR assistant secretaries who were career foreign service officers, Stape Roy and Phyllis Oakley. Stape, like Mort, had begun his career as a China specialist. Also like Mort, Stape had risen to the rank of career ambassador. By law, there can be no more than five career ambassadors at a time, and I worked for—and learned from—two of them. I worked for Phyllis Oakley twice, first when she was deputy assistant secretary for regional analysis in INR and again when she became head of the bureau. Phyllis's expertise was on South Asia, Africa, and nontraditional security issues such as population and migration, and she had served as deputy press spokesperson for the department. She taught me much about these regions and issues and helped me to work with the media.

I also worked for and learned much from the three other assistant secretaries for whom I worked in INR. Doug Mulholland was a career CIA analyst who headed the Intel unit at Treasury before moving to the State Department. Doug paved the way for my promotion to the senior executive service and fought successfully for my assignment to the senior seminar after I had been rejected as "overqualified" for the most senior training in the USG. During the ten-month-long senior seminar, I had the opportunity to work with officers from across the national security enterprise. The networking benefits that resulted served me well through the rest of my career. Toby Gati, a Russia specialist who had spent most of her career in academe and think tank settings, brought me to the INR front office as deputy assistant secretary for analysis in 1994 and gave me the daunting portfolio of "all countries and all issues" that I held, in various positions, for the next fourteen years. Toby's fanatical attention to evidence and clarity of argument, as well as her willingness to challenge what she (correctly, in my view) regarded as sloppy work by others made me a better leader. My last INR boss before I succeeded him as assistant secretary was Carl Ford, a career analyst who had served in DIA and CIA but had also held positions on the Hill and in the Pentagon. We almost always came to the same or similar analytic judgments, but we often got there by very different routes. With the exception of Doug Mullholand, I had known all of these mentors in different capacities over a number of years. Respect for one another's views and abilities made it possible to challenge ideas without making it personal and to stay focused on the fact that what we were doing wasn't about us. What it was—and should be—about was providing support to those we served and leadership to those we supervised.

I also benefited from the example, trust, rigorous demands, and high standards of many senior State Department officials. I learned to do better, and how to teach other analysts to be more useful, because they set the bar high, held me to account, and trusted me to protect what they shared in confidence. Those who were most influential, and most helpful, were Rich Armitage, Marc Grossman, Arnie Kanter, Tom Pickering, Colin Powell, Gaston Sigur, Strobe Talbott, and Larry Wilkerson.

To list all of the colleagues in INR and other Intelligence Community agencies would require almost as much space as is devoted to the substantive portions of the book, so I must limit the enumeration to those who were most influential, most helpful, or simply the best colleagues. Unfortunately, I know that I will omit the names of people who should be included, and for that I apologize. That said, I do wish to acknowledge the collegiality and contributions of: Jim Buchanan, Bob Carlin, Paula Causey, Chris Clarke, John Gannon, Steve Grummon, Sherry Hong, Sandi Jimenez, Chris Kojm, Dan Kurtzer, Wayne Limberg, John McLaughlin, Bo Miller, Joe Nye, Greg Treverton, and Bill Wood.

Much of the hard thinking about mission, structure, training, and collaboration reflected in this book was stimulated and shaped by the members of the senior team who helped guide analytic transformation after I became deputy director of national intelligence and chairman of the National Intelligence Council. I want to acknowledge in particular the contributions of Mat Burrows, David Gordon, Craig Gralley, Richard Immerman, Steve Kaplan, Jan Karcz, John Keefe, Ron Rice, Nancy Tucker, Mike Wertheimer, and John Wohlman.

Chapters 2 through 4 are revised versions of the Payne Lectures that I delivered at Stanford in 2009, and I am deeply grateful to the Payne family for funding that series and to Director of the Freeman Spogli Institute for International Studies and long-time friend and colleague Chip Blacker for suggesting that I use the lectures to explain some of the mysteries, misconceptions, and missions of the Intelligence Community to students, faculty, and other members of the Stanford community. The goal of those lectures, and of this book, is to enhance understanding of what intelligence analysts do and to inspire young people to consider careers in intelligence.

Finally, having saved the most important for last, I must thank my wife, Orlene, for her patience and unceasing good humor as I have dragged her around the world and spent too many late nights at the office during our more than four decades together. I simply could not have done what I did, both in terms of my career and this book, if I had not had her support, companionship, and ready laughter.

Reducing Uncertainty

1 REDUCING UNCERTAINTY

THE U.S. GOVERNMENT spends billions of dollars every year to reduce uncertainty. The National Weather Service spends more than $1 billion a year to forecast precipitation amounts, track storms, and predict the weather.[1] The Centers for Disease Control spend more than $6 billion to detect and investigate health problems in the United States and abroad.[2] The Departments of Agriculture and Energy track and predict production of crops and various types of energy.[3] Virtually every agency of the federal government monitors and forecasts a wide range of developments because farmers, manufacturers, state governments, travelers, and citizens in every walk of life want information that will enable them to make better-informed decisions about what to grow, whether to invest, and where to travel. In other words, we spend a lot of money to anticipate problems, identify opportunities, and avoid mistakes.

A substantial portion of what we spend to reduce uncertainty—almost $50 billion a year—goes to the U.S. Intelligence Community (IC).[4] The need for this amount of money is justified through a process that emphasizes threats to our nation, our interests, and our people. For example, the classified and unclassified versions of the Annual Threat Assessment submitted to Congress by the director of national intelligence devote far more attention to problems and perils than to opportunities to shape events.[5] This emphasis is understandable, but it is also unfortunate because it obscures one of the most important functions of the Intelligence Community and causes both analysts and agencies to devote too little attention to potential opportunities to move developments in a more favorable direction.[6]

Intelligence Community work to reduce uncertainty differs from that of other U.S. government (USG) agencies in a number of important ways. The most obvious, of course, is that it has access to clandestinely acquired and other classified information. Indeed, the IC exists, in part, to ferret out secrets and to collect information that cannot be obtained by scholars, journalists, bankers, diplomats, or other "collectors."[7] The use of classified information does not automatically make analyses produced by the Intelligence Community better than those produced using only unclassified information, but reducing uncertainty about a large number of traditional national security issues can be more precise and often more reliable if IC collectors have managed to intercept, inveigle, purchase, or steal information that others wish to keep hidden.

Another way in which IC efforts to reduce uncertainty differ from those of other USG agencies is that most IC products remain classified for a long time. The reasons they do include the need to protect sources and methods (that is, how we obtained the information), the value attached to objectivity and clarity (it can be difficult to obtain a hard-nosed assessment of a foreign political leader or military capability if the analysis is intended for public dissemination), and the fact that many IC assessments are used to determine policies and negotiating positions of the U.S. government (telling others what U.S. officials are considering before they have made a decision on the issue is generally thought to be unhelpful). Despite recurring assertions to the contrary, IC analytic products are not classified for long periods of time to prevent taxpayers from knowing what they get for $50 billion a year. Classification decisions are made when assessments are produced, almost always on the basis of the classification level of information used in the report. I cannot imagine a situation in which an analyst or manager would say, in effect, "This analysis is really bad. Let's disseminate it to decision makers but give it a very restrictive security classification so the public will not see how bad it is." In my experience, most intelligence assessments are not very sexy or exciting, and few present theoretical breakthroughs of any kind. But that does not mean that they are poorly crafted or of little value. As noted in Chapter 5, hundreds of National Intelligence Estimates have been declassified and released. Most of them stand up pretty well, especially if judged against the criteria of "Were they useful to decision makers at the time they were produced?" and "Did they help to reduce uncertainty—even if only by reaffirming what officials thought they understood to be the case—about issues being deliberated in the USG?"

Reducing uncertainty sometimes involves acquiring information, overtly and covertly, that is thought to be useful to understanding developments or intentions. Sometimes it involves research and analysis to produce what Carl Ford refers to as "new knowledge," that is, better understanding and new insights derived from thinking hard about information we possess but have not considered or combined in the way that led to the new assessment.[8] At still other times it involves efforts to substantiate or disconfirm a hunch articulated by a customer or fellow analyst or to refute statements made in a meeting or the media. Reducing uncertainty, in other words, can take many forms and involve many types of analysis, but it almost always strives to enhance understanding of what is known, what remains unknown, what is happening, where events seem to be headed, what is driving them, and what might alter the trajectory of developments.

Contrary to fictional depictions and popular misconceptions fueled by political grandstanding and media caricatures, the intelligence enterprise exists to do more than steal secrets and "connect the dots." Ferreting out information that adversaries wish to hide and discovering (and disrupting) terrorist plots and other threats to our nation and our interests are important missions and, disparaging characterizations notwithstanding, we perform them very well—most of the time. We never have batted 1.000 and never will, but getting it mostly right, most of the time, in time to shape, prevent, or prepare for developments with the potential to affect our nation, our citizens, and our interests is and will remain our most important goal and criterion of success. Unlike highly paid ballplayers, we will never be satisfied with a .300 batting average. The security of our nation requires that we come as close to 1.000 as is humanly possible, and every IC analyst worthy of the title is determined to do so, both individually and collectively.[9]

For reasons of patriotism, professionalism, and personal pride, Intelligence Community analysts aspire to meet exceptionally high performance standards. High standards, and high expectations, are intrinsic to the profession because how well or badly analysts perform can have real-world consequences. As I have told thousands of new recruits, they must always be cognizant of the facts that U.S. government officials will be influenced as well as informed by what they say and write and that the efficacy of U.S. policies and actions will be determined, in part, by the analysis they produce. For those who serve in the U.S. Intelligence Community, the often-derisive phrase "good enough for government work" has a very different meaning than it does in conventional usage. In the Intelligence Community, "good enough for government work"

means not simply that it must be as accurate as possible but also that it speci-
fies clearly what is and is not known about the issue, the quantity and quality
of available information, what assumptions have been used to bridge intelligence gaps, what alternatives have been considered, and how much confidence
analysts have in the evidence and their judgments.[10] It also requires addressing the right questions at the right time and ensuring that information and
insights are delivered to all the right people.[11]

The first list of requirements summarized in the previous paragraph involves tradecraft issues. In most respects, the requisites for good intelligence
analysis are identical to the requirements for good academic analysis and
good analysis of all other kinds, and IC analysts can—and must—rely heavily
on the analytic methods they learned in graduate school. There are differences
between academe and the world of intelligence (for example, deliberate efforts
to hide information and to deceive or mislead foreign governments are much
more common in the work of the Intelligence Community than they are in
academic research), but the differences should tip the balance in the direction of enforcing even higher standards for IC analysis than for peer-reviewed
academic papers.[12] In other words, I have no sympathy for arguments that
one must give IC analysts a break because they operate under conditions and
constraints that generally are not found in university or think tank research
settings. To the contrary, standards of performance for the Intelligence Community can be no lower and arguably must be higher than those in academe
for the obvious reason that the potential impacts of IC analysis are far more
consequential. An academic who does bad or sloppy work will be chastised
by peers and perhaps denied tenure, but faulty intelligence analysis has the
potential to redirect U.S. foreign or security policies, discredit or endorse the
positions of foreign leaders or governments, raise doubts about the loyalty of
citizens or corporate actors, or cause the United States to undertake unwarranted or counterproductive military actions.[13]

The second set of requirements previously noted—right questions, right
time, and right people—is more germane to intelligence analysis than it is to
academic research but has both similarities and analogs for certain types of
think tank research and for consulting firms producing analysis for particular clients. There are important differences, but the IC, think tanks, and con-
sultants all produce "targeted" assessments timed to inform—or influence—
particular decisions. All three produce other types of analysis as well, but my
focus here is on products that have been requested by a particular customer or
are produced at the initiative of an analyst or manager who knows the issue

and the target audience well enough to judge that examining a particular question or set of questions at a particular point in time would be helpful to the targeted decision maker.[14]

The line between analysis produced to inform and analysis produced to influence can be very vague and may exist mainly in the eye of the beholder, and many argue that intelligence analysts must stay far back from that line lest they be guilty or suspected of policy advocacy.[15] I certainly agree that intelligence analysts must not be advocates for policy and that they must be—and be seen to be—as objective as possible. That, as well as having access to classified information that is not available to most analysts outside the Intelligence Community, is what distinguishes them from the many other individuals and organizations pushing information and ideas to U.S. policy makers.[16]

Intelligence analysis is exacting work, but the intellectual and psychic rewards can be substantial. The challenge of unraveling a mystery, solving a geopolitical puzzle, or discovering previously unknown or unappreciated dimensions of situations with the potential to affect the security of our nation and the efficacy of its policies requires rigor, dedication, and flashes of inspiration. For an analyst, the process itself is enjoyable; producing an assessment that enhances understanding and assists those we support is very gratifying. Nevertheless, most of the time analytic achievements earn mainly—or only—psychic rewards and commendation from peers and immediate supervisors. Pats on the head or "attaboys" from those we support are much rarer than they should be. That is unfortunate but probably inevitable because the nature of intelligence support makes it an iterative process in which continuous interchange between decision makers and analysts clarifies issues, integrates new information into preexisting intellectual frameworks, and produces more incremental increases in understanding than "eureka" moments of discovery. The analyst plays a critical role in this process by providing new information and new insights, but the payoff comes when the decision maker takes ownership of the new idea. Having made it their own, customers seldom want to share credit unless they still have only low confidence in the idea or insight. Intelligence analysts must remember that the goal is not to make themselves smarter but to make those whom they support more knowledgeable about the issues they are working on in the hope that policy makers will make better decisions. In my experience, customers are more likely to show their appreciation for analytic assistance by asking more questions and granting greater access to deliberative meetings than they are to give analysts credit for providing an insight that triggered or facilitated new policy recommendations.

Solving analytic puzzles is more difficult than providing valuable input to those we support. Much of the time, we can be useful without being brilliant. As Carl Ford regularly reminded our analysts when he was assistant secretary of state for intelligence and research, on any matter of importance there are probably dozens of things that policy makers think they should know about the issue. Of the dozens of things they think it important to understand, they think they know only a few and actually understand fewer than that. This creates an enormous opportunity for analysts to provide valuable input. If they can generate new information and/or new insight on just one or a few of the things policy makers would like to know, they have increased understanding and reduced uncertainty. They may also have given the customer they support a bureaucratic advantage because if he or she understands the issue better than others working the problem, or at least is able to convince them that he or she understands it better, the likelihood of gaining deference or support for that customer's preferred course of action goes up.

Policy makers appreciate it when analysts give them information and insight that they can use to advantage as well as to deepen their own understanding, and they often reward utility with greater confidence and better access. That is natural and helps analysts to become even better informed about the intelligence and analytic needs of those they support.[17] Such a relationship should not—must not—lead to situations in which analysts provide new information and insight only to their primary customer. Analysts need the confidence and trust of those they support if they are to do their jobs effectively, but an important part of their jobs is to ensure that the insights they produce are provided to "everyone" working the issue and, an even more difficult challenge, to all who might find them useful. This means sharing their insights with analyst counterparts who support other policy makers, publishing them in widely disseminated publications, posting them on appropriate websites, and writing them at a level of classification that makes them easily accessible to all who might find them useful.[18]

CONTINUITY AND CHANGE

The purpose of intelligence since time immemorial has been to reduce uncertainty about the aspirations, intentions, capabilities, and actions of adversaries, political rivals, and, sometimes, partners and allies. What the recipients of intelligence support want to know about has changed greatly over the years, as have the means of collection, the pace of operations, and the amount of information available. But IC customers still want to avoid surprise and to understand developments well enough and soon enough to avoid, alter, or ameliorate potentially adverse consequences for national security and other national interests. Other continuities include the insatiable demand of customers and analysts for "more and better" intelligence; the persistence of information gaps that must be bridged using assumptions, analogies, and alternative hypotheses; and the critical importance of experienced analysts and sound tradecraft. The primary purpose of this book is to describe some of the changes that have transformed the scope, content, and time lines of intelligence analysis during the past two decades and, more importantly, to enumerate and explicate enduring requisites for the production of accurate, insightful, and useful analytic judgments.

A second purpose is to describe what analysts do, how they do it, and how they are affected by the political context that shapes, uses, and sometimes abuses the fruits of their labors in the analytic vineyard. The book is written from the perspective of one who has seen the process from the bottom, the middle, and the top, both within and across the diverse components that constitute the U.S. Intelligence Community. I know that there are important differences in the missions, customers, expertise requirements, and career paths of analysts in each of the eighteen analytic components of the community and have argued strenuously that it is imperative to respect and preserve most such differences.[19] It is even more important to integrate the capabilities that exist in different components of the IC and to capture synergies latent in its structure. The discussion of analyst roles and responsibilities acknowledges these differences but focuses instead on commonalities to underscore the points that analysts have more in common than they sometimes believe to be the case and that the requisites of good analytic tradecraft are essentially the same no matter where one works.

The third purpose is to enumerate some of the lessons that I have learned as a participant observer who began my intelligence career as an Army linguist and military analyst in 1970, became a senior manager of intelligence analysts in 1989, and was given the opportunity to lead the analytic transformation effort mandated by the Intelligence Reform and Terrorism Prevention Act of 2004[20] when I was named deputy director of national intelligence for analysis and chairman of the National Intelligence Council in 2005.[21]

This is, in many respects, a personal tale. I have decided to write the book in this way because analysts working in the Community today and, probably, for some time to come will be working within the parameters that I helped to establish during 2005–2008, and I believe it important to articulate why I did some of what I did during that period. The result is neither a personal nor an organizational history. It is spiced with anecdotes from my own career that helped shape my perception of what worked and what didn't, and it presents the approach to change that I employed when given the opportunity to lead the analytic community. This book recounts some of my thought process, the lessons I learned and attempted to apply, and some of the ways in which my decisions were influenced by the organizational and political environments in which I operated. For all of these reasons, the book is more analytic narrative than objective history. It makes no pretense to being a definitive account of change in the Intelligence Community or a comprehensive review of what has been written about the Intelligence Community by others. Indeed, most of the sources cited are intended to provide additional information or alternative views; inclusion does not necessarily signify endorsement, but the pieces cited may stimulate additional thoughts and challenges to what I have written or help to clarify points that receive only cursory treatment in this book.

EVOLVING AND ESCALATING EXPECTATIONS

The origins and objectives of the modern U.S. Intelligence Community date to the immediate post–World War II era and were designed, in important respects, to preclude "another Pearl Harbor."[22] For the most part, this required careful monitoring of the Soviet Union and its allies to guard against the possibility of a surprise attack by an alliance far more formidable than the Japanese empire was in 1941. We became very good at watching the Soviets, and they became very good at watching us. The purpose was clear, the focus was sharp, and there were no surprise attacks on the United States. After the Sino–Soviet split, the IC broadened its focus and became adept at monitoring multiple countries simultaneously. The key point I want to make here is that, for decades, the priority objective of the IC was to monitor threats from big nation-states.

That changed after September 11, 2001, when the focus for much of the work of the IC shifted from nation-states to nonstate actors, principally al Qaeda. It is much harder to monitor nonstate actors than it is to monitor the conventional and strategic forces of big countries. The criterion for IC success also shifted, from detecting plans or preparations for a military strike against the United States, its facilities, or its allies abroad to detecting plans and preparations for an unconventional attack on landmark buildings or other nonmilitary targets inside and outside the U.S. homeland. The task of the IC became more difficult in proportion to the shift from detecting an attack that would presage nuclear war endangering millions of people and our way of life to one that might be an isolated event endangering thousands of Americans. For smaller groups with lesser capabilities, the challenge was even greater.[23]

The aftermath of the failed 2009 Christmas Day airline bombing indicated that expectations and demands for the Intelligence Community had escalated again. Now the criterion for success is detecting the plans and preparations of individual malefactors capable of killing hundreds of Americans by destroying a single airplane.[24] Similar narrowing of focus has occurred with respect to other objects of security concern and requirements for IC attention. For example, it is no longer adequate to be able to pinpoint the location of all nuclear-armed missiles; now the Intelligence Community is expected to be able to pinpoint the location of individual terrorists, individual improvised explosive devices (IEDs), and individual shipping containers. In other words, one determinant of the number of "dots" to be collected and connected has expanded from a handful of big countries to literally billions of individuals located in almost 200 nation-states. The attendant escalation of expectations and demands for precision requires more than shifting focus or adding a few analysts. Using a mathematical formula as simplistic as the "connect the dots" metaphor, even if nothing else had changed (which was not the case), the transition from a few countries to billions of individuals made the challenge roughly a billion times more difficult.

The demise of the Soviet Union and end of the Cold War changed the equation and expectations in many other ways as well. One was to broaden substantially the scope of issues subsumed under the rubric of national security to encompass concerns—many now defined as "threats"—as disparate as the effects of global climate change, infectious disease, cybersecurity, trafficking in persons, counterfeit pharmaceuticals, and international criminal networks. Every one of these "new" threats/challenges/IC responsibilities is both important and difficult to monitor on a global basis. Broadening the scope in this way brought a number of new "customers" into the mix, and they, in turn, further expanded the number of questions and issues in the Intelligence Community's portfolio of responsibilities.

Broadening the scope of issues assigned to the Intelligence Community and increasing the number of customers and topics on which they wanted "more information" coincided with dramatic advances in technical collection and data management capabilities. Defense contractors and other vendors seeking new markets for products and services to replace those no longer needed in Cold War quantities happily embraced the Intelligence Community as a priority customer and produced even more dramatic gains in the ability to collect, process, and manipulate digital data. Analysts were, of course, delighted to have more information and more ways to store and manipulate data, but many were reminded of the admonition to be careful about what you wish for because you might get it. After years of pleading for "more intelligence," we got it—big time. Analysts are now awash in data, and there are literally billions of times more "dots" to be examined, evaluated, assessed, and integrated into analytical products. Those who speak glibly about "connecting the dots" seemingly have no idea how immense and difficult it is to perform what they often describe as a task so simple that children can do it.

Collecting information is a necessary but not sufficient condition for understanding our rapidly changing and increasingly interconnected world, and terabytes of data alone do not reveal event trajectories, what is driving them, where they are headed, what might derail or deflect them, or how they will interact with developments originating thousands of miles away. Making sense of the data and distilling insights helpful to decision makers are the responsibility of analysts. Stated another way, the role of analysts is to convert data into insight. We embrace this responsibility because it contributes to the safety, security, and success of our country. That is why intelligence analysts are paid to do what we do, and it is a very strong motivating factor. But it is not the only reason intelligence analysts work as hard as they do to unravel mysteries, solve puzzles, and discover new insights. In addition to patriotism and professionalism, most intelligence analysts I have encountered through the years are also motivated by the intellectual challenge and psychic rewards inherent in the job.

This is probably a good point in the narrative to make clear that the foregoing discussion of escalating demands and expectations should not be read as a complaint or lamentation.[25] At one level, it is simply descriptive. As a former colleague used to say, "It is what it is." Describing these dimensions of change is not intended to evoke sympathy for the plight of overworked and underappreciated analysts or simply to decry demeaning characterizations of what it is that intelligence analysts are supposed to do (that is, connect the dots). What it is intended to do is provide a succinct explanation of why working harder, adding more analysts, and simply tweaking time-tested IC practices would be woefully—and dangerously—inadequate to meet current and foreseeable requirements for intelligence support. To meet demands and expectations, the Intelligence Community must be transformed. This is, in important respects, a book about transformation. More specifically, it attempts to describe how I thought about the transformation of analysis that I was entrusted to lead. Each of the other chapters uses anecdotes and illustrations to indicate how I saw and experienced changing circumstances and lessons that I learned and applied while serving in the Bureau of Intelligence and Research (INR) and as deputy director of national intelligence for analysis. My reason for writing it this way is to describe what it is like to be an intelligence analyst and to explicate my own thinking on issues germane to reform in the hope that doing so will stimulate others to do the same and continue the transformation that was begun on my watch.

ORGANIZATION OF THE BOOK

This is a book about the roles and responsibilities of analysts in the U.S. Intelligence Community. As such, it says very little about collection, covert action, post–9/11 efforts to reduce barriers between foreign intelligence and domestic law enforcement, the creation of the Office of the Director of National Intelligence, efforts to transform the IC from a collection of feudal baronies into an integrated intelligence enterprise, or other important dimensions of intelligence reform. Nor does it focus explicitly or extensively on the collection of measures I supervised to build a community of analysts and thoroughly transform the way analysts collaborate, gain access to information, interact with persons outside the Intelligence Community, or broaden and deepen their expertise, as well as many other dimensions of the transformation agenda.[26]

The overarching objective of the book is to provide a sense of the constraints, challenges, and opportunities that Intelligence Community analysts confront at various stages of their careers. It does not present a "typical" career trajectory or enumerate requisites or formulas for success, mainly because there is no "typical" career trajectory, and describing patterns from the past is almost certain to be misleading with respect to the future. Indeed, because a central theme of the book is that we are doing and must do many things differently than in the past, it would be counterproductive to suggest that career choices and trajectories appropriate to a different time and different circumstances provide a useful guide for success under very different conditions.

The whole point is that old patterns are no longer adequate and that analysts must contribute to the transformation of almost everything associated with our profession.[27] Transformation must be achieved through a combination of evolution from the top and revolution from the bottom. This book is intended to stimulate creative thinking and innovation from analysts at all grade levels and in all agencies. It is also intended to increase public understanding of what IC analysts do and to elicit more relevant and constructive suggestions for improvement from outside the Intelligence Community.

Although the book does not offer a typical career trajectory, it does provide a series of anecdotes and examples to illustrate the kinds of challenges and opportunities that I experienced during the nearly four decades that I was a working analyst and a senior manager of analysts. My career was not typical, but the issues, pressures, and opportunities that I experienced are not at all unique, and the lessons I learned from the customers I supported and the colleagues on whom I had to depend, especially after my portfolio expanded to include "all countries and all issues," have broad applicability. One of the most important of such lessons was that I had no option except to rely on the work and judgments of my colleagues and subordinates. There simply was no time—and I did not have the requisite expertise—to review the intelligence used in more than a tiny subset of the roughly 14,000 analytic reports that I approved during eleven years in the INR front office and four years as chairman of the National Intelligence Council (NIC). I could review the tradecraft, but I could not check the homework. I had to trust the people who had done the work. Some proved to be more worthy of that trust than others, and one of my objectives in leading analytic transformation was to ensure that all analysts in all agencies were sufficiently well trained and well supervised that customers and colleagues could assume that all analysts employed good analytic tradecraft.

Each of the remaining chapters focuses on a different dimension of analytic work in the Intelligence Community. Chapter 2 examines some of the ways movies and other fiction have exaggerated and mischaracterized Intelligence Community capabilities, both to set the record straight and, more importantly, to make the point that public expectations about our ability to track individuals anywhere on the globe all the time have been skewed by media depictions of remarkable capabilities. Our "failures" to find Osama bin Laden or to know Iranian intentions are inexplicable and inexcusable in direct proportion to the extent to which the public thinks we are as good as Hollywood pretends that we are. Similarly, fictionalized versions of what we do and how we do it make it difficult for ordinary citizens to appreciate the magnitude of the challenges that result from increasing the range and number of intelligence customers, the scope of issues subsumed under the heading of "national security concerns," the amount and variety of expertise required to understand complex issues, and the precision required to make intelligence judgments "operational." Most of Chapter 2 focuses on the escalation of requirements and the challenges of coping with vastly more information in ever-shorter periods of time.

Chapter 3 focuses on the responsibility of analysts to convert data into insight and what is required to provide useful input to decision makers. Intelligence analysis involves more than just answering hard questions and solving puzzles when most of the pieces are missing. It also involves much more than connecting the dots. Unlike academic researchers who generally select what to study based on questions that interest them, have only loose or nonexistent deadlines, and take great pride in producing knowledge for knowledge's sake, IC analysts have an obligation (as well as an opportunity) to deepen understanding of issues affecting U.S. national interests and the safety of our citizens. Most of the time, their research agendas are driven by customer requirements (both formal requests and those requirements intuited by analysts who understand the issues and the policy concerns well enough to recognize when customers "need" information or insights that have not been requested) and decision time lines. Analysts seldom have time to research a problem thoroughly or to "get it completely right," but they always have an obligation to provide input germane to the issue in time to be useful. An analyst who figures it out after it is too late to inform debate and decisions has failed to be useful. This chapter is mostly about ways to be useful.

Chapter 4 addresses the perennial tension between current intelligence and strategic analysis with a primary focus on using analysis to anticipate and shape the future. The chapter also looks at why IC analysts pay more attention to threats than to opportunities and to warning about the possibility of bad things to the neglect of providing input that might help customers to increase the likelihood of positive developments. Strategic warning analysis is illustrated with examples from the NIC's 2008 study, *Global Trends 2025: A Transformed World*; the 2008 National Intelligence Assessment on the geopolitical effects of global climate change; and the 2007 National Intelligence Estimate, *Iran's Nuclear Intentions and Capabilities*. The first two case studies focus on the processes used to produce assessments and the political environment in which they were produced. This chapter also introduces the importance of identifying trends, what drives them, where they are headed, and what they might portend for U.S. interests. Each of these factors is examined at greater length in Chapter 5.

Chapter 5 focuses on estimative analysis, particularly National Intelligence Estimates—what they are, what it means to say that they represent the "most authoritative judgments of the Intelligence Community," why and how they are important, and why they have such high political salience and symbolic importance. The chapter also addresses other types of estimative analysis to underscore the apparently nonobvious point that preparing an estimate is what one does in the absence of data needed to make an exact calculation or assessment. Intelligence analysis almost always involves working on problems that are important, either intrinsically or because U.S. policy makers have defined them as important, and on which key data are missing. The more data are missing, the more dependent policy makers are on the assessments of IC analysts. This means, inter alia, that almost by definition—and most of the time—IC analysts must use assumptions, analogies, or alternative hypotheses to bridge information gaps. It also means that, most of the time, they will make errors and fail to pinpoint exactly what has transpired. Accuracy is desirable, but providing useful input that helps decision makers to deal with uncertainty is more valuable. Few estimates contain theoretical breakthroughs or reach surprising conclusions, but that does not necessarily detract from their utility at the time they were produced. Hundreds of declassified estimates have been released. Most of them were mostly correct.

The penultimate chapter, titled "A Tale of Two Estimates," narrows the focus from estimative intelligence in general to just the flawed 2002 NIE on Iraq's weapons of mass destruction and the controversial 2007 estimate on Iran's nuclear intentions and capabilities. Its central purpose is to describe factual and process errors in the production of the Iraq weapons of mass destruction (WMD) estimate, the lessons I learned from that experience, and how those lessons were translated into procedural guidance that shaped the Iran nuclear NIE. The chapter also examines how flaws in the Iraq WMD estimate influenced the intelligence reform legislation that created the Office of the Director of National Intelligence and mandated specific steps to improve analytic tradecraft. This is also the most politically focused chapter in the book in that it describes my interactions with members of Congress who took unprecedented interest in the Iran nuclear NIE as well as on my expectations for the way in which the Iran NIE would be scrutinized to determine how well the IC had learned the desired lessons from critiques of the Iraq WMD estimate.

ADDITIONAL BACKGROUND

Although, or because, this book does not examine in detail the objectives, logic, or specific measures of the approach to analytic transformation that shaped and were shaped by the topics and developments discussed in this volume, a brief summary of what I was attempting to do will help to put what follows into broader context. My rationale for not adding chapters on analytic transformation to this book is that I could not figure out how to do so without either losing the internal logic and focus of the book or producing something that looked like two different books held together by one cover. Nevertheless, I believe the short summary that follows provides a useful characterization of the what, why, and how dimensions of my approach to analytic transformation and makes it easier to understand why I have focused as I have on the topics discussed in each of the subsequent chapters.

The Intelligence Reform and Terrorist Prevention Act of 2004 mandated and facilitated the most extensive reform of the Intelligence Community since its creation in 1947.[28] As is often the case, members of Congress and many others seemed to argue that passing legislation had fixed the many deficiencies identified by the 9/11 Commission, the Senate Select Committee on Intelligence, and the WMD Commission.[29] President George W. Bush subsequently mandated many recommended measures that were not addressed in the legislation.[30] Together, these documents prescribed dozens of measures to improve analysis. I knew that I had to address all of them and that many were inextricably linked, but I also knew that they were not equally important, especially in terms of their political salience and that I could not possibly gain support for—or cooperation on—attempts to address all of them at the same time. To make the task more manageable, I adopted the approach summarized in the following paragraphs.

Rather than spend a lot of time trying to devise a comprehensive plan for analytic transformation, I decided to develop the plan iteratively by beginning with tasks that I knew had to be addressed and for which I knew I had considerable support among top managers of analysis across the Community. The decision to build the plan as we went along was motivated by the realization that I was unlikely to get it right the first time anyway, so there was no point in trying to devise a perfect plan before addressing problems that needed urgent attention, and by the judgment on my part that, if I put out a plan with any specificity, I would end up spending time and effort debating and defending the plan at the expense of discovering what worked, what didn't work, and what changes were needed to keep the process moving in the right direction. In short, my grand plan was to start small, fail cheap, fix problems as they arose, and build support by making managers across the IC active participants in the process. It became "our approach," rather than "my approach."

I decided early on that my highest priority had to be restoring confidence in the quality of our analytic work and the analysts who produced it. This was a nontrivial challenge because criticism of IC incompetence had been so sweeping and so damning that many customers who had no exposure to or experience with the Iraq WMD estimate began to wonder if the analysis they were receiving was any better, and many analysts lost confidence in their colleagues, their own agencies, and the Community as a whole. Unless we addressed this problem quickly, the IC—which in this case meant primarily analysts—would lose the confidence of and access to the policy customers they supported. Moreover, with the imminent departure through retirement of baby boomer senior analysts and the intake of large numbers of new analysts, we faced a possible staffing crisis if veterans decided to leave earlier and newly hired analysts decided that they did not want to work in an incompetent organization. A third dimension of this challenge was to build confidence in the quality of work done by colleagues in other components of the IC so that we could devise sensible divisions of labor, increase our analytic capabilities through collaboration across institutional boundaries, and reduce the amount of duplicative effort in order to assign more people to new problems.

Among the steps I took to restore confidence was to focus on early and visible improvement of the two flagship analytic products, the President's Daily Brief (PDB) and National Intelligence Estimates (NIEs). Director of National Intelligence John Negroponte had delegated responsibility for both to me, so I had the authority to mandate changes without having to go through cumbersome procedures needed to produce Intelligence Community directives and similar policy guidance.[31] Because it was the flawed Iraq WMD estimate that had triggered the campaign to improve analysis, I knew that estimates would receive especially close scrutiny, at least for a while, and that if we failed to demonstrate improvement there, we would be assumed to have failed elsewhere as well. Conversely, if we demonstrated improvement in National Intelligence Council products, we would be assumed to be making comparable progress elsewhere. The situation was similar with respect to the PDB. Very few senior officials saw the PDB, but they were the most important officials in the USG, and at least some of them had lost confidence in the Intelligence Community. If we did not regain their confidence quickly, we would become a hugely expensive irrelevance.

Using the PDB and NIC products as primary vehicles for demonstrating improvement also facilitated my plans to improve overall IC analytic performance by improving the performance of each of the analytic components of the community and to do that, in part, by improving the performance of analysts in each of the agencies. The adoption of common analytic tradecraft standards across the IC and training analysts to meet those standards were logical next steps. The enormous intake of new analysts that occurred after 9/11 created an imperative and an opportunity to ensure that all were trained to the new standards. This also created an opportunity for joint training, that is, training analysts from across the IC in the same classes to mitigate organizational cultural biases and build confidence among analysts based on knowing that counterparts in other agencies had received the same training.[32]

The final element of the strategy that I want to note here is the development of new norms of and mechanisms for collaboration across agency boundaries. The model for this was the "Korea Team" in INR. It was comprised of analysts from five offices scattered across three floors of the State Department who interacted primarily via email. In other words, they were a virtual team with members separated by space and bureaucratic divisions. Because electrons can move between buildings and cities as easily as between floors of the same building, we had a model for virtual collaboration. To facilitate virtual teams and collaboration at a distance, we had to change security restrictions impeding the sharing of information among agencies and to introduce capabilities better than email. I used collaboration on PDB drafts, which now had to be coordinated among agencies rather than merely within the CIA, as a forcing function; if the system was sufficiently secure to transmit the PDB, it was secure enough for other products. Subsequently we introduced Intellipedia, a classified version of Wikipedia, and, later, A-Space. Analysts took to the new collaborative tools very rapidly, perhaps owing in part to the large percentage of young analysts accustomed to collaborating at a distance.

There are many other components of analytic transformation, but the point I will end with here is that we had a fortunate convergence of opportunity, necessity, urgency, and enthusiasm that enabled us to gain traction and build momentum. There is still a long way to go, and many of the hardest problems have yet to be solved, but there is still widespread enthusiasm on the part of analysts and eager determination to provide the best possible analytic support to those who make decisions affecting the safety and security of our country.

2 MYTHS, FEARS, AND EXPECTATIONS

I ONCE BEGAN a public lecture by asking members of the audience, "How many of you collect or analyze intelligence?" When no hands went up, I asked, "How many of you interpreted the question as 'Which of you is a spy?'" That prompted a few to raise their hands and enabled me to ask, "What if I ask the question somewhat differently? How many of you check the thermometer before deciding what to wear? Or how many tune in to traffic reports before deciding what route to take during rush hour? Who checks the newspaper to find out what movies are playing and when they start before heading to the theater?" The answer, of course, is that we all do these things. We do them—as we do many other things—to inform our decisions and to make better choices. That, in a nutshell, is what intelligence is all about. The world's "second old-est profession" and our multibillion-dollar intelligence budget exist to reduce uncertainty, provide warning, and inform decisions, especially those related to the security of our nation and the safety of our citizens.

SCOPE AND STAKES

The questions I posed to my audience were intended to demonstrate that we all collect, analyze, and use intelligence. If you are uncomfortable using the word *intelligence*, you can substitute *information*, but that does not change the purpose or the process. Pro football teams, venture capitalists, epidemiologists, and many others routinely collect, analyze, and apply intelligence to increase the likelihood of success in whatever they are trying to accomplish. All such examples have much in common with the Intelligence Community, but there also are important differences of scope, expectations, and impact. Perhaps the greatest difference is their potential impact. The United States might act or refrain from taking action because of what intelligence analysts say or write. From my vantage point, much of what is written about the Intelligence Community fails to recognize the similarities or to understand the impact of the differences. As a result, the Intelligence Community is treated as more sui generis than it is, and, ironically, most proposals to make it better ignore or imperil those aspects that are, and probably should be, unique.

OMNISCIENT AND INCOMPETENT

Movies, spy novels, and the news media have shaped perceptions of Intelligence Community capabilities and competence. As a result, most of what you think you know about intelligence is probably wrong. Elements of the prevailing caricature can be summarized as follows: The Intelligence Community is comprised mainly of secret agents and computer geeks who know everything about everywhere all the time but are so incompetent that they cannot "connect the dots" despite huge budgets and reckless disregard for our civil liberties. Does that sound about right? Well, the description of the caricature may be fairly accurate, but the caricature itself is not. The Intelligence Community does do some pretty incredible things, but mischaracterizations and mythology frequently distort the challenges we face and the capabilities we use to reduce uncertainty.

Let me turn first to the question of whether we do, can, or should know "everything" that happens or will happen, anywhere in the world, all the time. Movies depicting "spy agency" video of truck movements and terrorist camps in North Africa or South Asia used to be pure fiction, but reality is catching up with artistic license.[1] Indeed, the use of video has become an essential element of force protection in Iraq.[2] But we cannot photograph everywhere all the time, and, even if we could, there would never be enough imagery analysts to make sense of what we had.[3] Having a picture is not the same as knowing the significance of what you can see. Two illustrations will clarify what I mean.

Until I mandated changes in tradecraft and procedure a few years ago, it was common for analytic reports to contain statements such as, "According to imagery, North Korea shipped missiles to Syria."[4] Such statements were misleadingly definitive. The imagery cited might show a wooden crate sitting on the dock of an identified port. A picture might be worth a thousand words, but a photo of a box on a dock doesn't tell you what is in the box or where it came from. Judgments about content, origin, and destination are based on information that clarifies the meaning of the image. In my experience, pictures seldom speak for themselves.[5]

The second illustration is from the infamous Iraq weapons of mass destruction (WMD) National Intelligence Estimate produced in 2002. Judgments about chemical weapons were based, in part, on assertions by imagery analysts that a particular combination of vehicles was the "signature" for the movement of chemical munitions. Pictures clearly showed canisters being moved, but the special truck in question was a water tanker—a fire truck—that was used for the transfer of munitions of all kinds. The chemical weapons analyst didn't know that, and those using the imagery-derived judgments did not have visibility into the underlying logic and evidentiary chains.[6] IC analytic managers have worked hard to correct that problem.

The cautionary note implicit in these illustrations should be self-evident, but commentary about connecting the dots and fantasy depictions of intelligence make it imperative to underscore the importance of analysts and their role in evaluating, assessing, interpreting, and explaining data obtained by spies, satellites, diplomats, journalists, scholars, and other collectors of information. I could have substituted the word *intelligence* for *information* because unclassified information—called "open source intelligence" in the jargon of Washington—is often as important or even more so than data acquired through stealth or espionage. This is certainly true with respect to good journalism, rigorous academic research, and firsthand disaster reports filed by law enforcement personnel, nongovernmental organizations, and persons working for international agencies. They are not spies, and what they report is not espionage, but it is—or can be—extremely important to Intelligence Community analysts attempting to understand complex and/or fast-moving developments.

Learning that a bridge has been destroyed in an earthquake and that planned routes for evacuation or provision of assistance cannot be used is valuable "intelligence" for first responders regardless of whether the information comes from a commercial satellite or a missionary with a cell phone.[7] Similarly, imagery collected by a commercial satellite or forwarded to a television network by a bystander with an iPhone can be just as useful as the product of expensive—and sometimes dangerous—clandestine collection. Moreover, no matter what their provenance, images and other forms of information must be interpreted by analysts. For example, a cell phone video of police beating a demonstrator (or demonstrators beating a police officer) sent to a cable news outlet must be assessed to determine whether the beating was staged for propaganda purposes. Doing so is the job of analysts. Some analysts work in the Intelligence Community, but most do not.

Before shifting from imagery to communications intercepts, a second commonly depicted and distorted collection capability, I want to underscore three points. The first is that our technical capabilities, though much less than imagined or imputed, are really very impressive and are rapidly becoming even more so. The second is that collection is often the easy part; interpreting what the collected information means can be extremely difficult and cannot be done without skilled analysts. We have more imagery—and other forms of intelligence—than we do analysts, and we already collect more than we can process. This is important because, until the information is processed in the mind of an analyst, it is just data. Third, the more we are able to do with imagery and other technologies, the more we are asked and expected to be able to do, proving once again that no good deed goes unpunished.

A similar situation pertains with respect to signals intelligence. We have big ears and can pull in huge quantities of digital data. Much of it is freely available—radio and TV broadcasts and websites, for example—and we make as much use as we can of publicly available information. The preferred option is—and should be—to use information that is accessible at minimal cost and no risk. On many subjects, there is no need to search beyond the troves of publicly available information, and it would be foolish to steal or buy what we can obtain for free. On other subjects, corroborating what is available in open sources with clandestinely acquired information is important to increase confidence in the accuracy and validity of the information.[8]

On a relatively small number of issues, however, such as terrorist plans, illicit transfers of biological agents, or black market arms sales, most of what we need to know can be obtained only by using clandestine collection. As is the case with imagery, there are very exaggerated views of how much we collect and what we do with the information. Exaggeration is not limited to the movies or the media; for years the European Parliament has issued studies and warnings about a U.S.-led collection of voice and fax traffic that it calls "Echelon." According to these "studies," the United States and our partners collect virtually every phone call.[9] We don't. Even if we could, we wouldn't want to. It would take tens of millions of analysts to process the data, yielding a result that would be mostly dross. Can you imagine spending your entire day listening to teenagers on their cell phones? We want to know the ultimate destination of terrorists who have completed their training in South Asia and departed for Europe or North America, not what one fifteen-year-old thinks about another's boyfriend.

It is important to underscore three additional issues related to the collection and exploitation of voice and other forms of communication. The first is volume; even if it were possible to collect everything, it would make no sense to do so because we would be drowning in data, the vast majority of which would be completely irrelevant to any conceivable national security objective. The days of gathering up "everything we can" on the chance that the metaphorical drift net would pull in something of value are long gone. To give you a sense of why this is impractical, think about the challenges of finding something of value in a potential cache of information that increases in volume equal to the holdings of a major research library every few hours. The actual magnitude gives new meaning to the expression "drowning in data." The only sensible approach is to begin with a focused question and then design collection strategies to answer the question, ones that promise to provide the greatest insight into specific policy concerns, be they diplomatic strategies, military intentions, or the capabilities of a new antitank gun.

The second issue concerns civil liberties and the right to privacy. This issue achieved high salience and sparked passionate debate in 2006–2007. Much of the debate was focused on so-called warrantless wiretaps.[10] The underlying issue was a serious one, but it was grossly distorted in the partisan political arena. This is a subject that warrants further discussion, but the point I want to make here is that respect for our rights as Americans is both a personal concern for our intelligence professionals—we are Americans too—and the subject of strict legal and procedural regulation.[11] Show a veteran foreign intelligence professional a report with the name of an American citizen or entity, and he or she is likely to react as if it were radioactive; you can go to jail for spying on Americans. But clear and long-established procedures for handling information on Americans were changed after 9/11 with the goal of breaking down barriers between law enforcement and foreign intelligence that had impeded detection of the 9/11 plot.[12] It should come as no surprise to anyone that domestic law enforcement materials are loaded with information on Americans— how do you tell the police who to watch if you can't provide a name? How can you check for links between domestic criminals and foreign organizations if you can't share a name? The result was a real dilemma—or, more accurately, a series of dilemmas—for the Intelligence Community. To cite just one: Was it better to err on the side of protecting the civil liberties of individual Americans or to lean forward in alerting officials to possible terrorist or other threats to the homeland? The "default setting" for most professionals was to err on the side of civil liberties, but doing so raised disturbing "what if" questions. Civil liberties protection officers and formal boards exist to ensure that fear and zeal do not erode the liberties our national security enterprise exists to protect and they do an excellent job.[13] But this is a daunting challenge.

INTELLIGENCE "FAILURES"

I will shift gears now and take up the question of "intelligence failures." One of the lessons I learned early on in Washington is that there are only two possibilities with respect to national security policy, "policy success" and "intelligence failure." You will search for a long time to find a public statement describing what has happened as a policy failure that occurred despite an intelligence success.

Policy makers sometimes make "bad" decisions, but they can always claim—and often do—that they made the bad decision because the blankety blank (fill in the expletive of your choice) Intelligence Community failed to anticipate, discover, interpret, and explain a situation adequately. This is obviously self-serving, but, in some ways, the syllogism is true. If the Intelligence Community does not provide adequate warning, misses key developments, misinterprets the available information, and/or uses bad assumptions and inappropriate analogies to close information gaps, it isn't providing the quality of support for which it was created and receives a great deal of taxpayer money. That intelligence misled policy makers is certainly the impression many have—and many others want you to have—of the relationship between the publication of the 2002 National Intelligence Estimate on Iraq's weapons of mass destruction and the decision to overthrow the regime of Saddam Hussein. I have a different view, but my purpose in citing that estimate here is to illustrate broader points about the relationship between intelligence judgments and national security decisions. My take on shortcomings and lessons of the Iraq WMD estimate can be found in Chapter 6.

INTELLIGENCE AND POLICY DECISIONS

The first point I want to make in this context is that intelligence usually *informs* policy decisions and sometimes *drives* the decision making process, but it does not and should not *determine* what is decided. This point warrants repetition: Intelligence usually *informs* policy decisions and sometimes *drives* the decision-making process, but it does not and should not *determine* what is decided. By *informs*, I mean that intelligence is just one of many streams of input flowing to national security decision makers. Others include formal and informal input from Cabinet members and NSC staff, the media, lobbyists, old friends, foreign officials, powerful members of Congress, and so on.[14] Most of the time, the goal of the nonintelligence inputs is to argue for a particular decision or course of action, such as sending military assistance to Georgia after the August 2008 military clash with Russia or mounting a public diplomacy campaign to discredit Venezuelan President Hugo Chavez. At other times, it is to put pressure on the president and/or other senior officials to stop deliberating and "do something" to stop the killing in Darfur or human rights abuses in Burma.

Intelligence is not supposed to—and in my experience very seldom does— advocate specific courses of action. Its primary purpose is to provide information and insight that will enhance understanding of the core issue, how it relates to other matters, and possible consequences of alternative courses of action. Stated differently, the primary purpose of intelligence inputs into the decision-making process is to reduce uncertainty, identify risks and opportunities, and, by doing so, deepen understanding so that those with policy-making responsibilities will make "better" decisions. Being better informed does not guarantee better decisions, but being ill informed or misinformed certainly reduces the likelihood of policy success.

Sometimes intelligence *drives* as well as informs the decision-making process. One way that it does so occurs when collectors discover—and analysts assess—something new that simply cannot be ignored. For example, I remember working very hard over a weekend in 1988 after we determined on a Friday that China had delivered CSS-2 missiles to Saudi Arabia.[15] Among the reasons for the crash analysis was the need to provide input to Secretary Shultz, who was scheduled to meet with China's foreign minister the following Monday. The meeting had been scheduled for weeks to discuss other issues, but the new intelligence judgment put missiles on the agenda. The Intelligence Community wanted more time to figure out what had happened and why, but in such cases no administration official wants to explain to the Congress why the issue was not raised at the earliest opportunity. Potential or actual pressure from Congress is a subset of a broader category of ways in which intelligence sometimes drives policy and presses officials to make decisions or take action. Another, and more infuriating, source of pressure is the leaking of intelligence information, usually in a way that overstates what is known, downplays or ignores different interpretations of what it means, and imputes a degree of reliability that may be completely unfounded.

The value of intelligence, and here I mean primarily analytic judgments on the reliability, meaning, and implications of information obtained from publicly available and clandestine sources, is a function of both the rigor of the analytic tradecraft employed and the confidence officials have in the quality and objectivity of the judgments. Both dimensions are important because even high-quality assessments will have little impact if officials lack confidence in the Intelligence Community. I used the Iraq estimate as a starting point for this discussion because when postinvasion searches failed to locate any weapons of mass destruction, administration officials, members of Congress, and career professionals in national security agencies lost confidence in the quality of work done by all analysts on all subjects, not just Iraqi WMD. Job One for me after I was named deputy director of national intelligence for analysis in 2005 was to restore confidence in our work and our people. We succeeded. That is not just my assessment; it is what I was told directly by the president, our congressional oversight committees, the President's Intelligence Advisory Board, and senior officials across the policy community.

BOUNDING—AND FULFILLING—EXPECTATIONS

The Intelligence Community is a can-do organization, but it cannot do everything. Over the course of the last twenty years, four phenomena or streams of developments have interacted in ways that severely stressed the ability of the Community to provide the level and types of support required to satisfy escalating and expanding demands for information and insight. The first is the *can-do attitude* itself. Support to policy makers and military commanders has a very long history and is integral to both the ethos of the Community and the professionalism of its members. Individuals and each of the sixteen constituent agencies of the Intelligence Community play different roles, support different missions, and apply different types of expertise, but all are deeply committed to the security of our nation and the safety of our fellow citizens. Among other consequences, this predisposes all of them to accept and attempt to answer any question or request. There is great reluctance to dismiss requests for help on grounds that the subject is not an intelligence priority or is outside the bounds of traditional national security concerns, even if it requires information and expertise that the Intelligence Community does not have. This is laudable in many ways, but it is also hazardous and unsustainable.

The second stream of developments results from the *escalation of requirements and demands* assigned to or assumed by the Intelligence Community. As noted earlier, the post–Cold War era has seen dramatic changes in the scope of issues subsumed under the rubric of national security. In the much simpler—but more dangerous—days of the Cold War, "all" we had to worry about was the existential threat to our nation and our way of life posed by the Soviet Union and its allies. The target was big, slow moving, and predictable. Over the decades, we became very good at watching the Soviets. We spent years developing capabilities to penetrate specific targets, acquiring essential skills, and building a large cadre of people with the linguistic, technical, political, and other areas of expertise needed to address a single, overriding threat. Almost everything else was relegated to secondary or lower priorities. This was well understood across the federal government, and demands and expectations for the Intelligence Community were modulated accordingly.

That was then. Over the last twenty years, requirements and expectations have grown exponentially. Paraphrasing former Director of Central Intelligence Jim Woolsey, we once focused most of our attention on one big dragon, the Soviet empire; now we have to deal with thousands of snakes of various sizes and lethality, many of which may not be dangerous at all.[16] The increase in the scope of what we are expected to "know" came about for many reasons but mostly because we—three presidential administrations, the Congress, and the American people—redefined the scope and meaning of national security. You can see the evolution quite clearly if you skim the unclassified versions of the Annual Threat Assessments (sometimes called Worldwide Threat Assessments) presented to the Congress every year as part of the budget justification process.[17]

Two decades ago, the reports focused on strategic threats to our survival as a nation—nuclear annihilation, conventional warfare, and the development and proliferation of various kinds of weapons. That changed. In testimony that I delivered in January 2001, and in parallel testimony by Director of Central Intelligence George Tenet, we declared terrorism to be the greatest threat facing our country.[18] In contrast, Director of National Intelligence Dennis Blair's 2009 statement for the record presenting the coordinated views of all components of the Intelligence Community declared the global financial crisis to be the primary near-term security concern. The Soviet Union no longer exists, nuclear war has receded as a concern, former adversaries have become NATO allies, and China is viewed as both economic partner and competitor. The list of threats now includes the effects of global warming, the spread of infectious disease, the price and availability of oil and natural gas, and a host of other topics that were once considered beyond the scope of national security concerns.[19]

The dramatic expansion of the scope of intelligence requirements and concerns did not occur simply because the Intelligence Community was looking for something to do after the demise of the Soviet Union. There may have been some of that—the Intelligence Community was reduced by roughly 25 percent in the 1990s—but from my vantage point as a senior official, the most significant drivers were new concerns and objectives articulated within the executive branch and/or the Congress. As policy makers realized that they needed to know more about a host of challenges and opportunities that had not made it onto the radar screens of their predecessors, they turned to the Intelligence Community. I suspect that the main reason they did so was because we were there. That, and because we are essentially a "free good" at the disposal of officials who do not have to cover our costs from their own budgets. Because we have a strong can-do culture, because we shared the sense that it was necessary to redefine the scope and content of "national security concerns," and possibly because some were eager for a new mission, we accepted the new requirements and began providing input on the widening range of subjects.

I will interrupt the evolutionary narrative to illustrate the kind of questions we are now being asked by citing an example from my own direct experience. It occurred in 1994 in the aftermath of appalling ethnic violence in Rwanda that resulted in the death of some 800,000 people in the space of two months. At one point, approximately 200,000 refugees from the violence escaped into western Zaire (now the Democratic Republic of Congo) and collapsed in exhaustion in an area known as the Valley of Death, where the international community geared up to provide food and shelter. The area was at the foot of an active volcano spewing toxic fumes and apparently on the verge of another eruption.[20] Aid officials faced a dilemma: If they tried to relocate the exhausted and dehydrated refugees too quickly, many would die; if they left them there, they might be killed by flowing lava or noxious gasses. The question directed to me was, "When will the volcano erupt, and, if it does, which way will the lava flow?" That was not a traditional intelligence question, and I wasn't going to get the answer by tapping Mother Nature's telephone. But we did get an answer. Bill Wood, the geographer of the United States who worked for me in the Bureau of Intelligence and Research, went to the U.S. Geological Survey, which put us in touch with specialists on the Nyiragongo volcano. The volcanologists judged that in the next eruption, lava would flow down the side of the volcano away from the camp. That input, which we obtained in a matter of hours, influenced the decision not to relocate the camp and the exhausted refugees. This example illustrates both the nature of new intelligence questions and the need to develop networks of experts inside and outside of the Intelligence Community.

The third stream of developments affecting expectations regarding what the Intelligence Community can do—or should be able to do—derives from what I would characterize as a *shift in focus from the security of the nation to the safety of individual citizens.* The terrorist attacks on 9/11 underscored and intensified this shift, and one can make a convincing argument that it has gone too far. The point I want to make here, however, is that the criterion for evaluating government success and Intelligence Community performance has been elevated from detecting, deterring, and/or defeating any threats to the survival of our nation and way of life to one that comes pretty close to detecting and preventing harm to every American, anywhere in the world, all the time. To state the change in this way is, of course, to overstate what has happened—but not by much. The Intelligence Community has a long history of focusing on the intentions and capabilities of other nations and foreign leaders. We still do that but must also identify, penetrate, and monitor very small groups of potential terrorists who might attack a school or shopping center in the United States—or a U.S. embassy or American citizens working for an international NGO on the other side of the world. This shift was illustrated by the criticisms leveled at the Intelligence Community after the failed attempt by Umar Farouk Abdulmutallab to detonate his "underpants bomb" on a December 25, 2009, flight to Detroit.[21]

The redefinition of national security to encompass the fate of individual Americans and U.S. facilities is reflected in the Intelligence Reform and Terrorism Prevention Act of 2004. That legislation redefined "national intelligence" and "intelligence related to national security" to include to all intelligence, whether gathered inside or outside of the United States, that involves threats to "the United States, its people, property, or interests." Quite apart from the civil liberties concerns, which are real, raising the bar from "threats to our national survival" to "threats to the safety of all Americans" imposes enormously more difficult requirements on the Intelligence Community.

The final stream of developments contributing to the escalation of expectations regarding the Intelligence Community involves what I will call *time compression*. In the good old days of the Cold War—and yes, I know that they really weren't so good—we had weeks, months, and years to find and follow potential threats. For example, when the Soviets built a new missile submarine, we often knew about their intention to do so, watched the keel being laid, and monitored the sub's subsequent construction, departure for sea trials, relevant missile tests, and eventual operational deployment. While that was happening, my kids went from kindergarten to high school. Not only did we have a long time to study phenomena of concern, we (happily) almost never had to act on the intelligence beyond developing countermeasures and even better monitoring systems. There was plenty of time and opportunity to make course corrections as we learned more about the problem. That, too, has changed.

Now a large and still growing percentage of what we do must conform to very short decision time lines. Here, too, there are many causes and manifestations. One is the twenty-four-hour news cycle. If something happens, or is reported to be imminent, policy makers seemingly feel compelled to comment or to demonstrate that they are on top of the issue. Before doing so, they frequently go to the Intelligence Community with some variant of the "Is that right?" question. "I'll get back to you next week" is not an acceptable answer. Among other consequences, this means that we need both a very large reserve of "fire extinguishers"—analysts and collection activities providing "global coverage" with at least a watching brief so they can quickly get up to speed when needed and/or can provide an informed response to short-fuse taskings. It also means that we need to develop and maintain extensive networks of "outside experts" knowledgeable on particular subjects, willing to share what they know with the U.S. government, and sufficiently attuned to the pace and other requirements of Washington to provide timely and targeted input to a process that simply cannot wait.

The need for speed is compounded by the need for expertise. The Intelligence Community has a formal and quite effective process for establishing priorities. We use the prioritization framework primarily to guide collection, but it also affects budgets and the number and experience of analysts assigned to different topics. Despite the prioritization of topics, we must, as noted above, maintain sufficient coverage of "everything" to be able to respond quickly. We also need to maintain sufficient expertise to be able to interpret and assess complex phenomena in a very short time. The onset of a crisis is not the best time to begin to collect basic data, establish baseline descriptions, identify outside experts, and formulate alternative hypotheses to explain observed phenomena and close information gaps. Maintaining the requisite levels of expertise on literally thousands of topics is a major challenge. This challenge is made more difficult by demographics: More than 50 percent of Intelligence Community personnel joined the government after 9/11. Think about that and the implications of having to deal with more and harder questions and the need for speed. The resultant challenges and dangers are both obvious and substantial. But that isn't all.

In addition to having less time to wrestle with more complex problems than ever before, we must meet higher standards for accuracy and precision. In the jargon of our profession, we need to provide more "actionable intelligence." It is no longer good enough to know that an adversary is building a new military installation that will take months or years to construct, giving us plenty of time to learn more about it. Much of what we did in the past played out on that kind of timeline and amounted to a form of intellectual voyeurism. Now, the requirements for force protection, avoidance of collateral damage, interdiction of drug traffickers, and so on require far more precision and errors are far more exposed. I will cite just a few more examples.

The first involves a Chinese ship named the *Yin He*. In 1993, we obtained intelligence—considered to be extremely reliable by the collectors—that the *Yin He* was transporting a particular chemical to Iran. The chemical was on a list of proscribed items, and the new Clinton administration wanted to block delivery. Our ambassador in Beijing asked the Chinese government to look into the matter and was subsequently told by President Jiang Zemin that the ship was not carrying the proscribed chemical. The collectors stood by the accuracy of their information, and the Saudis agreed to search the ship during an intermediate stop. China specialists in the Intelligence Community and the State Department insisted that searching the ship was a bad idea because Jiang would not have said what he did unless he was certain that the chemicals were not there. Well, we searched the ship and didn't find anything. This too could be the subject of a long discussion, but here I want simply to note that we are still suffering the consequences of that misguided interdiction effort because the Chinese and many others cite the *Yin He* episode almost every time we tell them we have intelligence that something untoward is about to happen and request their assistance.[22]

The second example involves the incident in 1999 when the United States mistakenly bombed the Chinese embassy in Belgrade. According to the database used for targeting purposes, the Chinese embassy was located some distance from the site targeted, which was thought to be a military warehouse. The database was out of date. Many in China, and around the world, believed at the time and continue to believe today that the attack was deliberate. It wasn't, but the error illustrates the high bar for accuracy that we must meet every day.[23] The point is further illustrated by the debate about collateral damage from military operations in Afghanistan.[24]

I will close with one more story that illustrates many of the points I've attempted to make in this chapter. In the mid-1980s, I was part of the skeleton crew working in the State Department on a Saturday morning when I discovered an intelligence report that the Communist Party of the Philippines planned to blow up an unnamed tourist hotel in Manila. According to the report, the bomb would explode in slightly more than one hour. After trying unsuccessfully to reach a Philippine analyst, I took the report to the senior East Asia officer on duty. He framed his choices as follows: If I urge the government to evacuate the hotels and no explosion occurs, I will undercut the tourist economy and the credibility of the new government. If I don't do that and a bomb explodes, people will die, and we will have failed to do anything to prevent it. He looked at me and said, "Is the report true? Your call will determine what I do." I swallowed hard and answered that such an act would be inconsistent with my understanding of the modus operandi of the communists in the Philippines and that I did not think it was true. He thanked me and alerted his boss and our embassy, but not the Philippine government. Then we both waited nervously for the deadline to pass. Thankfully, nothing exploded.

That kind of situation was relatively infrequent then; now it is repeated almost daily. One can argue about whether I should have erred on the side of safety by taking a "prudent" worst-case approach, but I simply note in passing that worst-case scenarios almost never happen and crying wolf has real consequences.

3 SPIES COLLECT DATA, ANALYSTS PROVIDE INSIGHT

IT WOULD BE an exaggeration to describe intelligence analysts as the Rodney Dangerfields of the Intelligence Community, especially so given the esteem and confidence that many have earned from the officials with whom they interact on a regular basis.[1] Nevertheless, even officials who respect—if not admire—the work of "their" intelligence analysts often join the chorus of voices seemingly eager to denigrate or dismiss the contributions of analysts in general. In that regard, and perhaps only in that regard, analysts are like members of Congress who are reviled as a group but often well regarded by their own constituents.[2] I suspect that the same phenomenon can be found in evaluations of many other professions (for example, auto mechanics or beauticians or whomever is described as terrible in general, although "my" mechanic is thought to be exceptionally good) but confess that I have not attempted to determine if such is really the case.

Such distinctions are understandable; if you think your representative or auto mechanic is terrible, why do you continue to vote for her or to take your car to his shop? Something similar might be at work in the distinction officials make between the positive assessment of their intelligence support team and intelligence analysts in general, but I think more is involved than a simple defense mechanism. Intelligence analysts earn the confidence and respect of those they serve by demonstrating knowledge, utility, and discretion.[3] Analysts who do not manifest these characteristics are likely to—and should—be dismissed or ignored by those they "support." In my experience, that rarely happens. I choose to believe that the reason it happens infrequently is that most analysts are pretty good, and the process whereby they are assigned to specific customers works pretty well, most of the time.

Analysts, like members of Congress and other professions, earn respect one at a time, but unlike for members of Congress, there is no mechanism to evaluate collective performance. The media and other watchdog groups regularly inform the public about the accomplishments (or lack thereof) of the legislative branch, but there is no similar mechanism for the Intelligence Community (IC). The fact that the vast majority of work done by analysts in the IC is classified and remains so for years precludes external review of the sort used to evaluate many other professions. Moreover, the scope of work produced by intelligence analysts is enormous, covering thousands of topics and tailored to meet the often very different requirements of several hundred customers. Devising meaningful metrics and methods for assessing overall performance might not be impossible, but it would be extremely difficult and, more to the point, would be of dubious value. What we really want—and need—to know is how well individual analysts and analytic units perform. We also need to know the relative efficacy of different analytic methods, tools, and forms of collaboration. The Intelligence Community has taken important steps toward continuous evaluation, but much more can and should be done.[4]

The paucity of objective, comprehensive, or even meaningful evaluations of overall performance has not precluded judgments about how well—or badly— IC analysts perform. Lacking other criteria, critics, commentators, and members of Congress have been quick to condemn all analysts for the sins of a few. I refer here specifically to the way in which all IC analysts—approximately 20,000 people—were tarred with the brush of criticism that was quite legitimately applied to the work of the dozens of analysts who produced the badly flawed 2002 National Intelligence Estimate on Iraq's weapons of mass destruction.[5] In saying this, I do not mean to disparage the excellent work of the Senate Select Committee on Intelligence and the WMD Commission, or to imply that all analysts who did not contribute to the Iraq estimate were completely innocent of the shortcomings identified in their studies. Indeed, I agree that the problems identified were quite widespread in the analytic community and that the critiques were a very useful motivator to correct long-standing deficiencies. The formal reports were not the problem; it was the way in which they were cited by commentators to disparage the capabilities and integrity of all analysts and to imply that the job of analysts is no more demanding than simply "connecting the dots." Being an analyst in the U.S. Intelligence Community is far more demanding than such caricatures imply.[6]

Caricatures and critiques implying that IC analysts—all analysts—are incompetent sting, even when one knows they have little basis in reality. I readily admit that I am not a disinterested or wholly objective commentator; I am an analyst and, more to the point, I spent most of my career as an analyst and manager of analysts in the U.S. Intelligence Community. Experience and direct knowledge of the people and processes involved doubtless cause me to be overly sensitive about criticisms I consider overstated or mean spirited. But my point here is not to complain about misinformed or misanthropic criticism or its negative effects on morale. It is simply, but importantly, to note that such criticism has a badly corrosive effect on confidence in—and the confidence of—the analytic community.

Despite the title of this chapter, it will focus almost exclusively on the roles and responsibilities of analysts. What collectors do is extremely important; analysts could not do what we do as well as we do without the information obtained by our colleagues in the collection disciplines. But, as noted, I am an analyst. Although I spent thirty-eight years in and around the Intelligence Community, I am not now and never have been a spy. Spies do important, sometimes incredible work, but without skilled analysts, much of what spies and other collectors do would have little value. Spies collect information, but until that information is assessed and interpreted by an analyst, it's just data. The pages that follow are intended to provide an overview of how analysts assist decision makers, military commanders, and other "customers" in the national security enterprise by providing information and insights that reduce uncertainty about what is happening, what is likely to happen, and what can be done to ensure or prevent specific developments.

THE ROLE OF ANALYSIS IN
THE NATIONAL SECURITY ENTERPRISE

The primary purpose of intelligence is to reduce uncertainty and clarify what we do not know about the issues confronting those who make decisions affecting our nation. Knowing more and having better understanding of the issues and drivers that shape events does not guarantee good decisions or successful policies, but it does improve the odds. The mission of intelligence analysis is to evaluate, integrate, and interpret information to provide warning, reduce uncertainty, and identify opportunities. Providing insight on trends, the political calculus of particular foreign leaders, or the way problems are perceived by people outside the United States is often more helpful to decision makers than is the presentation of additional "facts" or speculation about "worst-case" possibilities. Discovering that a country is cheating on a treaty commitment may be less important than providing insight into why it is doing so. Ferreting out all details of an adversary's new weapon system may be less useful than finding a vulnerability that can be exploited. Prompting decision makers to rethink their own assumptions and preliminary judgments may be more beneficial to the national security enterprise than providing definitive answers to specific questions.

Of the senior officials with whom I was privileged to work, the one who was most knowledgeable about intelligence and the Intelligence Community was Colin Powell. In one of our first conversations after he became secretary of state—at the time I was acting assistant secretary for intelligence and research—he gave clear and succinct guidance when I asked what he wanted from his in-house intelligence unit. That was, "Give me insight, not news." Later he met with everyone in the bureau and provided equally pithy and valuable guidance: "Tell me what you know. Tell me what you don't know. And tell me what you think." I have repeated that guidance many times but add one additional requirement, namely, "And make clear which is which." I learned a few years later that Powell had been giving this advice to intelligence officers for many years.[7]

Collectors provide input, often very valuable input, for the "what you know" basket. Analysts generally describe everything in the "what you don't know" basket as a "collection gap," but blaming the collectors is not an acceptable way to deal with the problem. The "what you think" category subsumes a number of distinct and equally important elements. One is explication of the assumptions used to close information gaps. Taxpayers do not spend billions of dollars on intelligence in order to elicit "we don't know" as the definitive statement about national security issues. We have to do better than that, and we do. Explicit articulation of assumptions—often to include identification of alternative assumptions (or hypotheses), and explication of why they were rejected—is part of the analytic process.[8] "What you think" also subsumes analytic judgments about what is driving events, where they are headed, what might deflect the current trajectory, how others will respond, and similar insights useful to policy makers and other customers.

A judgment is not a fact. A third component of "what you think" is the articulation of confidence levels—telling customers how much or how little confidence you have in the information available to you and the judgments you have made. Sometimes clear statements about the level of confidence are even more important than the judgments themselves, especially if the confidence level is low.[9] Confidence in the judgment logically should be lower if you know that other analysts, using the same information but perhaps different assumptions or weighing the evidence differently, have come to a different conclusion. Policy makers deserve to be—and now must be—told as soon as it becomes clear that analysts using good tradecraft have reached different judgments regarding important issues. The message policy makers should hear is, "Please note that the ice under this judgment is thin. Before you commit your prestige or the power of the United States to a course of action predicated on what intelligence analysts have determined to be the case, you need to remind yourself that available information and good tradecraft were inadequate to determine with confidence what has happened or what will occur." The need to make absolutely clear the existence of such analytical differences, and why they exist, is one of the clearest lessons learned from the postmortem on the much-criticized estimate on weapons of mass destruction in Iraq.[10]

Intelligence, especially analytic support, is useful to decision makers in direct proportion to the degree to which it is timely, targeted, and trusted by those who receive it. Another way to say this is that in addition to being factually accurate, intelligence analysis must be—and be seen to be—both objective and germane to the needs of those for whom it is intended. Thorough examination of all relevant factors and how they interact is seldom possible within the real-world decision timelines of U.S. officials, and getting it completely right is often less important than providing useful information and insights to the right people at the right time. Even data rich and methodologically brilliant analytic products may contribute little to the national security enterprise they are supposed to support if they are prepared without understanding of the knowledge, timelines, and objectives of officials working the issue.[11]

The Intelligence Community supports "all" of the agencies and individuals responsible for protecting our nation, our citizens, and our interests. Those expecting support cover a spectrum that runs from the president to the people who design equipment, tactics, and countermeasures for the Navy; formulate diplomatic strategy; or respond to humanitarian emergencies. The specific needs of individual and institutional "customers" depend on their bureaucratic responsibilities. For example, the Pentagon focuses primarily on military matters, but Treasury concentrates on economic issues, and the State Department is responsible for diplomacy and Americans living or traveling abroad.[12] The intelligence needs of these and other U.S. government organizations are very different. The desk officer responsible for Venezuela or Thailand needs qualitatively different intelligence support than does the secretary of state or the assistant secretary for Africa. As a result, intelligence support is a retail activity that must be tailored to the specific needs and timelines of individual customers. One-size-fits-all solutions are not very helpful to anyone.

The importance of tailored intelligence support has been apparent to me for many years, and I often assume that it is self-evident to everyone. That appears not to be the case, however. As a practitioner, I had time to read only a small subset of the critiques of and prescriptions for improving IC analysis but was struck by how little attention was devoted to this issue, especially in comparison to the amount of attention given to the simplification of organization charts and eliminating duplication of effort. There is no question that reducing the number of agencies and subgroupings within agencies would reduce cultural and bureaucratic impediments to information sharing and collaboration. Those are desirable goals, as is the quest for synergy and reduction of unnecessary duplication. But they are neither the only nor the most important objectives of intelligence reform. The most important goal must be to be useful to those we support, and being useful requires detailed understanding of what specific customers want to accomplish, what they already know, what they want to know, what they think they know that is erroneous, and what other players—usually limited to other nations or nonstate actors—know about and want to do about the objectives of that customer. It also requires detailed knowledge about decision time lines of one's primary customers and sensitivity to developments that could affect the goals and responsibilities of that customer set. In other words, to be truly useful, intelligence support must be tailored, timely, and trusted. All three require frequent and close interchange between intelligence analysts and those they support.

Intelligence analysts support their primary customers by helping them to cope with the unrelenting stream of issues, demands, and opportunities they confront every day. No matter what the specific job or portfolio, things happen—or are reported to have happened—that require attention, information, and understanding sufficient to determine whether they require the immediate personal involvement of a particular official or can safely be delegated or ignored, at least for the time being. No official likes to be in the position of not knowing about a development cited by a counterpart or raised by a member of Congress or the media. At a minimum, customers expect to be informed—or alerted if the development seems to be within their bureaucratic purview—but they always want more than notification that something has occurred or is about to happen. Collectors—those who elicit, purchase, steal, or stumble on information—can provide the "heads up," but analysts are needed to provide context, assess implications, and anticipate how events will unfold.[13]

A portion of every analyst's job involves answering questions. Sometimes the questions are posed in the course of a meeting and may require both an immediate answer and a longer and more considered response. Questions can be factual (for example, "When was the last time that North Korea staged military exercises as large as those now taking place?"), analytic ("Why did Iraqi President Maliki decide to move against insurgents in Basra without informing the United States?"), or estimative ("What is likely to happen in Afghanistan over the next six months?"). Factual questions are answered as quickly as possible, often on the spot. The ability of an analyst to provide confident answers with adequate levels of detail is a function of both expertise and ability to anticipate what the customer is likely to require. The adequacy of the response depends, in part, on the confidence those present have in the analyst.

Perhaps the best way to demonstrate the importance of reputation and trust is to provide a brief example from my years in the State Department's Bureau of Intelligence and Research (INR). As is normal in Washington, the electoral victory of George W. Bush in 2000 resulted in the return to office, usually in more senior positions, of people who had served in previous Republican administrations. One of the returnees was Richard Armitage, who became deputy secretary of state in the new administration. I had worked with Armitage in both the Reagan and the George H. W. Bush administrations when I was chief of the China division and, subsequently, director of analysis for East Asia and the Pacific, and our shared interest in Asia frequently brought us together at conferences and think tank–sponsored events during the years that he was out of office. As is often the case in Washington, previous and recurring encounters had engendered friendship, respect, and mutual trust that forestalled awkwardness and suspicion between political appointees and career public servants and smoothed the transition from one administration to another. I respected and trusted Rich, and he had confidence in my abilities as an analyst. Even though both of us now had global portfolios, our shared experience working on Asia in general and China in particular formed the foundation of the relationship.

Armitage's trust and confidence in my abilities as a China analyst became relevant in ways neither of us had anticipated following the April 2001 midair collision of a U.S. Navy EP-3 surveillance aircraft and a Chinese fighter. The Chinese pilot was killed, but the U.S. plane landed safely on the Chinese island of Hainan. The accidental collision created a potential crisis in U.S.–China relations while the new administration was still settling in.[14] Assistant secretary of state for East Asia and the Pacific (EAP) designee Jim Kelly had not yet been confirmed, and a number of other key positions in the State and Defense Departments were filled by career officers who were not well known to senior members of the administration. As acting assistant secretary for intelligence and research, I was directly engaged in efforts to assess what had happened and what might be necessary to secure the return of the crew and, if possible, the plane. Armitage wanted me to take an even more direct role as an analyst and in the development of a diplomatic strategy. This was not the time or situation to invoke hoary doctrines of separation between analysis and policy making. We—the United States—had a serious problem, and we—those with relevant experience and expertise—had responsibility for finding a solution.

I knew the career officers who were working the problem, and I had great confidence in their abilities. Under other, less stressful or potentially less consequential circumstances, simply attesting to their abilities might have been sufficient to reassure the deputy secretary, but that was not going to be the case in the first days of the potential crisis, and I knew better than to try. To make a long story short, after two days of blurring the roles of analyst and policy maker, I was confident that we understood what needed to be done to resolve the problem and, more importantly, was certain that my friends in the EAP Bureau understood this as well as or better than I. It was at that point that I felt able to say to Armitage that he could trust the acting assistant secretary for EAP (Darrell Johnson) and his team and did not need me to look over their shoulders.

The point of this anecdote is not toot my own horn as a China specialist but to illustrate the importance of trust, personal relationships, and sensitivity to the challenges and concerns of those we support. Armitage did not need me to solve the problem, but he did need me to give him confidence that the team of people he did not know well were up to the job and did not have a political agenda different from that of the new administration. I confess that I liked being a China analyst again (it had been seven years since I had assumed a global portfolio), but I had to remind myself continuously that I was out of shape and had to rely heavily on analysts and policy makers who worked China issues on a daily basis. In other words, I had to trust and have confidence in the quality of their assessments.

Sometimes the most important answers are the ones that address questions customers should have asked but didn't. To be useful, analysts need to know what their customers know, what they are trying to accomplish, and the approach being used to formulate and evaluate policy options. Questions that are more difficult to address include those that come to an analyst indirectly with little or no information on why the question was asked. The objective in all cases is to provide more than "just the facts." Good tradecraft requires providing information on context, patterns, the quantity and character of intelligence germane to the subject, and other insights likely to help customers to understand the issues that prompted the query. Three keys to providing timely and useful answers are command of one's portfolio, knowledge of where to go for data and help to interpret what it means, and practicing good analytic tradecraft even on routine or quick turnaround matters.

Answering questions is, in certain respects, the easy part of the job. Tracking developments germane to the analyst's own accounts and the responsibilities of his or her customers is more difficult because it requires asking the right questions and knowing where to seek answers. Although both customers and analysts routinely lament the existence of "collection gaps" and the paucity of information on specific subjects (when in doubt, blame the collectors!), on virtually every subject of any importance, there is a steady stream of information that might be relevant. One of the most important parts of an analyst's job is to formulate questions that will provide timely insight and can be answered with available or obtainable information.

Every analyst also has a responsibility to monitor developments and trends in his or her portfolio to determine where they seem to be headed and how they might affect American interests or the viability of approaches being considered or implemented by those they support. Analysts should also be alert to potential opportunities for policy intervention to mitigate or capitalize on what is taking place. For most analysts, most of the time, the focus should be on providing strategic warning, that is, informing customers what appears likely to happen far enough in advance to allow deliberation and the formulation of policies to encourage what appears desirable and to thwart or mitigate unfavorable or dangerous developments.[15]

Despite the rhetorical priority assigned to strategic warning, no official likes to be surprised by breaking developments or to appear out of the loop, even on matters outside his or her own portfolio of responsibilities. To avoid surprise—and embarrassment—they expect to be informed of new developments by multiple mechanisms, including their own staff or agency operations center, telephone calls from the field or a friend, or even TV and the Internet. But they assume, and expect, the Intelligence Community to function as a fail-safe alerting mechanism, and, if they are not alerted to breaking news, blame is usually ascribed to the Intelligence Community. Knowing this, analysts and the IC as a whole are conditioned and structured to monitor developments everywhere and to report events that make it over a relatively low threshold. Analysts also know that customers expect more than just the facts. They want to know what the facts mean.[16]

The combination of customers who do not want to be surprised and IC analysts eager to satisfy their primary customers is perhaps the most significant cause of what many have criticized as an excessive preoccupation with "current intelligence."[17] Many analysts complain about, and many pundits decry, the amount of time and effort consumed by the preparation of duplicative quick turnaround assessments of inconsequential developments and erroneous information. The problem is more insidious than simply wasting the time of many analysts. Assessing, explaining, and interpreting developments have a tendency to inflate their significance and thereby cause an individual, organization, or even the entire national security enterprise to become distracted by matters they cannot affect and do not matter all that much anyway, at least not to the security interests of the United States. Examples of such distractions include reports that an unsavory African rebel leader has moved across an international border from one ungoverned space to another, the fifth (or tenth or whatever) report that Venezuelan President Hugo Chavez is providing money to the same left-wing candidates in South American countries, and reports in unreliable foreign media that something untoward has occurred or will occur in another country.

WHAT POLICY MAKERS WANT AND WHAT THEY NEED

As a group, policy makers—and their counterparts in the military and law enforcement arenas—are smart and knowledgeable about the issues in their portfolios. Not all fit this characterization, but most do. Officials who have not had prior experience working with the Intelligence Community often begin their tenure by saying something like, "Just bring me the raw intelligence, and I'll figure it out myself." "Raw intelligence" or "traffic" is Washington jargon for information provided by collectors. Analytic products are referred to as "finished intelligence." The distinction significantly understates the difficulty and importance of what collectors do. Many decision makers doubtless are—or could be—good analysts, especially those with decades of experience, but most quickly discover that they simply do not have time to wade through the reams of information that pour in every day and that they have no real option except to let the analysts with whom they work serve as their eyes and ears on matters in their portfolio and do most of the heavy lifting to validate, evaluate, explain, and interpret the information that comes in "automatically" or in response to their own queries and analysts' instructions to collectors.

Some officials are refreshingly honest. When he was deputy secretary of state, Strobe Talbott asked me to stay behind when others left a briefing by analysts from an agency that shall remain nameless on developments in one of the Central Asian states that had been part of the Soviet Union. Before asking for a paper on a few aspects of what had been briefed, Talbott said, "I know people think I know all this stuff, but I really don't. I didn't want to hurt their feelings, but I had no idea what they were talking about." The analysts involved had violated one of the first rules of customer support: Know your customer. Know what your customer knows, what he or she wants to know, and what he or she doesn't seem to know that the analyst thinks that customer should understand. Such knowledge requires frequent contact and mutual trust. Talbott had also violated an equally important rule by not asking the analysts to explain what they had glossed over on the assumption that he already knew it. For the relationship between analysts and customers to work as it should, and as it often does, both parties must have sufficient confidence in the other to expose what they do not fully understand as well as what they really want to know. Though it is tempting to assign equal responsibility for the success of such relationships, and greater effort is now being made to educate policy makers in the art of making optimal use of their intelligence support team, analysts bear a disproportionate share of responsibility for making the relationship work.[18] When all is said and done, policy makers can—and do—make decisions without input from IC analysts, but analysts without customers who trust them are a waste of taxpayer money.

To earn the trust of those they support, analysts must demonstrate substantive expertise, objectivity, understanding of the mission and objectives of their customer, and discretion. All four of these elements are essential. Unless an analyst demonstrates mastery of the subjects in his or her portfolio, policy makers are unlikely to pay much attention to proffered insights or suggestions to think about an issue somewhat differently. Carrying "secrets" in a locked pouch enables an analyst to gain access, but unless the analyst can hold a sophisticated conversation on subjects germane to the responsibilities of the customer, he or she doesn't contribute much to the decision-making process. Objectivity is even more important because an analyst who is perceived to have an agenda will be assumed to be cherry-picking information and skewing analytic judgments. Failure to understand what the customer needs and is trying to accomplish degrades the utility of the information and insights provided by the Intelligence Community. Simply stated, if what is provided isn't relevant, it isn't useful. Working sufficiently closely with the customer to understand his or her requirements exposes the analyst to issues, options, and political strategies subsumed under the rubric of "the deliberative process." It requires both good judgment and discretion to distinguish what must be shared with others in the Intelligence Community to provide appropriate support to the national security enterprise as a whole from what must be treated as privileged information.[19]

Confidence and trust are essential because without them analysts can only guess at what their customers need, and policy makers will have scant basis for determining whether insights provided by IC analysts are better or worse than those from their own staff, foreign counterparts, interest groups, the media, or other sources of information.[20] Intelligence judgments should not automatically trump others, but they should be—and be seen to be—informed by as much or more information than other assessments, the product of rigorous tradecraft, and as objective as possible. This is especially true of what may be the most important judgments of all: those conveyed on the spot by trusted analysts who have the confidence of those they support. As already noted, reputation and integrity matter.

Many who write about the Intelligence Community with little understanding of how it actually functions insist that analysts must avoid becoming "too close" or "captured" by the officials they support. That admonition is right, but it is too vague to be helpful. As I have tried to make clear throughout this chapter, it is imperative that analysts be sufficiently close to their customers to understand their needs and gain their trust. How close is "close enough," and how close is "too close"? The answer depends on the personalities involved, their awareness of the role that each plays in the national security enterprise, and the professionalism of the analyst.[21] I have high confidence in the professionalism of IC analysts. We tend to be fiercely protective of our integrity, objectivity, and independence, and I trust most analysts to do the right thing, seek guidance when unsure, and report any attempt to "politicize" their work. The legislation that established the Office of the Director of National Intelligence mandated creation of an ombudsman for analytic integrity and a report to the Congress on instances of attempted politicization.[22] I'm happy to be able to report that the survey of all analysts that we conducted each year produced very few cases of perceived attempts at politicization, and that in most cases analysts also reported that they and/or their agency had taken appropriate steps to ensure that the attempts were unsuccessful.[23]

This might be the place for a few more anecdotes to provide a sense of the way things actually work. When I was chief of the China Division—way back in the Reagan administration—many people speculated about the difficulty I was likely to have when Gaston Sigur moved from the National Security Council to the position of assistant secretary for East Asia and the Pacific. They did so because I was thought to be further to the left than I am, and Sigur was considered by some to be extremely conservative. What actually happened is that we quickly developed an exceptionally close working relationship with a high level of mutual trust and affection. Gaston gave me tremendous access to his meetings and his thinking and regularly asked me to comment on papers prepared by his staff or ideas that he was thinking of proposing. I'm confident that he was looking for more than a "liberal" perspective; he wanted a sanity check to ensure that what was proposed was not wildly inconsistent with available intelligence and IC judgments, and he wanted to know what I thought about the region we both knew well. The highest priority for both of us was to protect and advance the interests of our country. I never thought I was in danger of violating my responsibilities as an analyst and am certain that the Intelligence Community was able to provide better, more focused support because of the optic into his thinking afforded by our relationship of trust and respect.

The second illustration is an exchange I had with Secretary Albright after I had briefed her on new information regarding a country in the Middle East. When I finished, and after she had asked a few factual and analytic questions, she said, "What should I do about this?" I replied, "Madame Secretary, I'm an analyst; you know I don't do policy." She said, "Right, and I don't do analysis. Now, what should I do?" I demurred a second time, saying that I didn't think I knew enough about her objectives and the broader policy context to provide an informed answer. Her response: "Tom, I asked your opinion because

I respect your judgment. That doesn't mean that I am going to do what you suggest, but I do want to know what you think." In response, I framed the problem as I thought it should be considered and suggested a course of action to deal with the problem. Having given a recommendation, I resolved to be even more careful to ensure that I did not select or interpret information obtained thereafter with the goal of validating or reinforcing my answer. I hope and expect that every analyst would do the same under similar circumstances.

DESCRIBING THE PROCESS: HOW SAUSAGE IS MADE

If the discussion thus far seems complicated, you have been paying attention. What you should have absorbed so far is that literally hundreds of customers spread across most components of the U.S. government are working thousands of issues simultaneously and levying an unrelenting stream of requirements on the Intelligence Community. Analysts turn for help to collectors who use overt, covert, and clandestine methods to obtain information that might help analysts to understand what is going on so they can provide insight to policy makers, military commanders, and other customers.[24] The process does not work as efficiently as it should, and we can and will make it better, but rationalizing the process is more challenging than you might expect, not just for reasons of bureaucratic inertia, truculence, and the like, but also because, despite the chaotic elements, the system actually works pretty well.

How do analysts discern the needs of their customers and provide insights useful to their roles and responsibilities? To answer that question properly would require fairly detailed descriptions of how several different analysts have modified general guidelines to fit the particular needs of specific customers. In other words, there is no single best method or key to success, and what works in some circumstances will not work in others. That said, it is possible to think of the exercise as involving two modes of interaction that occur simultaneously and are not mutually exclusive. The descriptive labels were invented for this essay, but the phenomena they describe are real.

Formal or *"coordinated"* support encompasses the products and procedures used to ensure that the most senior officials working national security issues have access to a common set of assessments and insights produced by Intelligence Community analysts. Though it is an oversimplification, you can think of this group as the White House and Cabinet-level participants in National Security Council–led endeavors. Each member of this group gets both a common set of products and briefings and tailored analytic support from his or her in-house intelligence component (such as INR in the State Department) and from analysts at the CIA (and sometimes other agencies) who support NSC "principals." "Principal" is Washington jargon for the senior official in any of several settings. This "core" of common information consists almost entirely of analytic assessments but sometimes includes selected pieces of "raw" intelligence that analysts think it important to call to the attention of senior customers.

This information is provided through the President's Daily Brief, which is a process as well as a product; National Intelligence Council products; and certain commissioned or independently generated analytic products germane to the subjects under consideration. These products have been subjected to rigorous quality control reviews and "coordinated," either formally or informally, among all appropriate elements of the IC. When analysts employing good tradecraft reach different conclusions, the process ensures that all—in reality seldom more than two—alternative judgments are presented in a balanced way. This was not always the case in the past, but it was built into the process after the sad experience of the 2002 estimate on weapons of mass destruction in Iraq. Knowing that senior officials are busy, travel, and have more to read than they can manage, the process provides three (or more) shots at the judgments, arguments, and insights of IC analysts. Key materials are presented (briefed orally and/or made available in hardcopy) through the PDB process, in briefing books prepared for meetings at which the issues will be discussed, and in a brief oral summary of Intelligence Community views presented during the meeting by the director of national intelligence or another IC "principal."[25]

Less formal and more highly targeted support is provided through regular interaction between subordinates of the "principals" (for example, undersecretaries, assistant secretaries, and below) and their IC support teams. These teams typically consist of one or two individuals who are included in meetings, know agendas and deadlines, and know what their customers know, want, and need as well as how they want to receive information (orally, in writing, via their own subordinates, and so on). The support team also includes a small number of analysts from the CIA or another "external" component of the analytic community. Ideally, the internal members of the team keep the external participants up to speed, but, frankly, that does not happen nearly as often or effectively as it should.

WHEN IT ALL COMES TOGETHER

At the conclusion of the old and rather bad TV show called *The A-Team*, George Peppard would always say, "I love it when a plan comes together." That often was the way that I felt about the performance of the Intelligence Community. Disparaging the work of IC analysts by citing the same list of "failures" is a game that anyone can play and many do, but the fact of the matter is that things go right, and we get it more or less right, far more often than not. Of the roughly 14,000 analytic pieces that I sent to senior officials in the years after I became deputy assistant secretary of state for analysis in 1994, only a handful turned out to be seriously flawed. Most were not completely correct, but they were useful to those we supported. And remember, the IC doesn't—or shouldn't—work easy problems with abundant evidence and minimal time pressure. We exist to do the hard stuff, to figure out what the puzzle looks like when we have only a handful of pieces and are not even sure that they all came from the same puzzle.[26]

My point here is not to defend accuracy or adequacy; it is to proclaim and defend the efficacy of the process I have outlined in this chapter. When the process works, which it does most of the time, it is far more elegant and important than the making of sausage analogy suggests. When it works properly, the following things happen:

- Senior officials across the national security enterprise receive the same core set of information, most of which is analysis focused on the issues they are currently working or will have to address together. This essential core includes the most carefully prepared and coordinated analysis produced by the Intelligence Community. When analysts interpret information differently or reach different judgments, the existence of—and reasons for—the differences are made known to all senior officials.
- Seniors and subordinates across the national security establishment also receive information and analytic input tailored to their own agendas and responsibilities. Here, also, substantive analytic differences are made known as soon as they have been identified.
- Seniors obtain sufficient information from their IC support teams to judge whether characterizations and options sent to them by subordinates are consistent with intelligence judgments on the issues.

- Submissions from subordinates should be, and usually are, consistent with intelligence judgments because the process is designed to ensure that those lower in the chain receive tailored intelligence support and have opportunities to query and task the analysts whose job it is to see that their customers have what is required to work a problem and that they know what information is being provided to those higher in the system. As papers move upward through the system, there are numerous opportunities for more senior policy officials to assess the appropriateness and viability of proposed actions in light of their understanding of the situation, which, in turn, has been informed by their own interaction with IC analysts. They will also know what information has been shared with other policy makers and with the Congress.
- Papers and proposals are informed by intelligence input that makes very clear what is known, where gaps exist, the assumptions used to close those gaps, the confidence analysts have in both sourcing and specific judgments, and whether (and which) alternative hypotheses or explanations were explored and considered to be less persuasive.

When everything works, which, again, is most of the time, there are no surprises as ideas move through the system. There are repeated opportunities to check on both the nature of the analytic judgments and whether policy recommendations are consistent with those judgments, and decisions are better than they otherwise might be because of the input provided by IC analysts. If something makes it all the way to the top of the bureaucratic food chain before a Cabinet officer or NSC senior director spots a glaring inconsistency, something has gone badly wrong.

In closing let me underscore that it is policy makers, not intelligence professionals, who decide what to do with the information and insights derived from information collected and assessed by the Intelligence Community. Most of the time, decisions and actions are clearly or broadly consistent with the intelligence judgments, but that is not always the case, and the discrepancies are not always bad. Policy makers are supposed to weigh factors in addition to intelligence, and this sometimes leads them down paths different from those suggested by the logic of analytic input. Intelligence professionals need to understand and respect that this is the way our system is supposed to work.

4 USING INTELLIGENCE TO ANTICIPATE OPPORTUNITIES AND SHAPE THE FUTURE

REDUCING UNCERTAINTY is usually interpreted to mean ferreting out secrets that adversaries wish to keep hidden and providing warning that will enable policy makers, military commanders, or law enforcement personnel to prevent or prepare for developments that threaten our country, our citizens, or our interests. This interpretation is not wrong, but it is too narrow. Properly conceived and applied, intelligence collection and analysis also identify opportunities for decision makers to shape the future by reinforcing positive trends and redirecting those headed in a problematic or negative direction. In theory, providing warning and anticipating opportunities are two sides of the same coin because both require deep understanding and close monitoring of developments in groups, countries, or issue areas. In theory, if one understands the situation, where events are headed, and what is driving them, it should be just as easy to identify opportunities to nudge things in a positive direction as it is to spot signs of trouble. The theory is sound, but priorities, practical considerations, and concerns about "politicization" cause the Intelligence Community to focus more attention on discovering and analyzing problems than on finding possible solutions.[1]

Attaching greater importance to detecting threats than to discovering opportunities is understandable, given the origins and, for many, the raison d'être of the Intelligence Community.[2] It may also be inevitable because of the linkage between "threats" to our nation and budget allocations for national security. A substantial portion of what we spend to reduce uncertainty—more than $50 billion a year—goes to the Intelligence Community. The need for this amount of money is justified through a process that emphasizes threats. For example, the classified and unclassified versions of the Annual Threat Assessment submitted to the Congress by the director of national intelligence devote far more attention to problems and perils than to opportunities for positive change.[3] This emphasis is understandable, but it is also unfortunate because it obscures one of the most important functions of the Intelligence Community and causes both analysts and agencies to devote too little attention to "good news" and potential opportunities to move developments in a more favorable direction. Each of these points warrants brief elaboration.

Despite its size, funding, and can-do attitude, the Intelligence Community (IC) cannot do everything that customers demand or desire. Requests and requirements have to be prioritized, and the IC has a rather elaborate process to review and rank order the approximately 9,100 cells in the matrix created by arraying roughly 280 international actors against thirty-two intelligence topics that have been grouped into three categories by the National Security Council.[4] When I was given responsibility for the process known as the National Intelligence Priorities Framework, almost 2,300 issues had been assigned priorities higher than zero. My first instruction was, "Reduce the number." I simply could not keep a straight face while attempting to justify 2,300 "priorities." We reduced the number substantially, especially in the two highest priority categories, but it is still very large because policy makers need—and expect—intelligence support on a great many issues.

Doubtless reflecting a widespread conviction that it is more important to identify and prevent bad things from happening than to find opportunities to effect positive change, the process used to winnow requests to a manageable number focuses more attention on threats than on opportunities. The resultant guidance to collectors and analysts has real-world consequences for what is targeted, what is collected, what is processed, what is analyzed, and what analysts look for. The net effect is that opportunities receive less attention than do threats.

Even with the consequences of a prioritization process biased in favor of threats, good analysts often have sufficient expertise and insight to identify opportunities to change the trajectory of events.[5] Unfortunately, many are reluctant to write up their findings. Their reluctance stems, in part, from incentives and disincentives in the evaluation process ("Why are you spending time on low-priority issues?"), but it also reflects concern that they might be perceived as attempting to make or change policy by recommending alternatives to existing policy. The "theoretical" distinction between pointing out opportunities and recommending policy is clearer than the real-world constraints imposed by the imperative to be as objective as possible and to ensure that analysis is not skewed to support one's preferred policy option. For many analysts, the "prudent" course is to keep their opportunity insights to themselves.

That they do so is unfortunate because their expertise and experience sometimes make them better able to see opportunities than can the policy makers they support. Moreover, policy makers regularly state that they want the IC to identify opportunities as well as problems, and, in my experience, most of them really mean it.[6] The key, much of the time, is development of a relationship of trust between the analyst and the policy maker that allows for dispassionate discussion of possibilities and policy alternatives. Without such trust, it doesn't happen.

TYPES OF INTELLIGENCE

Commentary on the Intelligence Community often draws a distinction between "current" and "strategic" intelligence, usually to decry excessive attention to explaining the latest intelligence factoids obtained by collectors and inadequate attention to longer-term strategic analysis. Such criticisms are valid, but they generally miss (or misrepresent) important points. One error is to underestimate the demand for what the military calls "situational awareness."[7]

Policy makers throughout the government want to know what is happening in their geographic and/or substantive areas of responsibility. No official wants to be caught by surprise by a colleague, foreign counterpart, or member of Congress who seems to know more than the official does about what is happening in his or her own portfolio of responsibilities. Even if the development in question is of almost no intrinsic importance, failure to know about it will be embarrassing and perhaps politically fatal. Washington can be a tough town. To prevent surprise and embarrassment, policy makers expect their own staff and their Intelligence Community support team to ensure that they are always "on top of" their own portfolios. This is the demand-side "pull" for current intelligence. There is also a supply-side "push" from the IC support team. Knowing that their ability to provide timely, targeted, and useful intelligence support to their primary customers requires winning and maintaining the customer's confidence, IC analysts err on the side of providing more "current intelligence" than necessary. Some policy makers will say, from time to time, that they would welcome more long-range analysis, but the unspoken caveat is that receiving it should not come at the expense of constant situational awareness.

Even though policy makers often are so consumed by the demands of their in-box and immediate policy issues that they have little time or appetite for longer-term developments, the pundits who proclaim the need for more "strategic" analysis are right. In the grand scheme of things, it is far more important for the Intelligence Community to reduce uncertainty about what might happen in the future than it is to ensure that policy makers know what has happened in the last few days or hours. Indeed, it can be argued that the most important justification for having an intelligence enterprise is to provide "strategic warning" sufficiently far in advance that policy makers can act to prevent, ameliorate, or capitalize on the anticipated developments.[8]

ANTICIPATING THE FUTURE

As Yogi Berra is said to have observed, "Prediction is hard, especially when it's about the future." But prediction is not—and should not be—the goal of strategic analysis. Rather than telling policy makers, "This is what will happen, so you better prepare for that outcome," strategic analysis treats the future as neither inevitable nor immutable. The goal is to identify the most important streams of developments, how they interact, where they seem to be headed, what drives the process, and what signs might indicate a change of trajectory. Stated another way, strategic analysis seeks to identify the factors that will shape the future so that policy makers can devise strategies and formulate policies to maintain positive trajectories and shift negative ones in a more positive direction. The ultimate goal is to shape the future, not to predict what it will be.

Strategic analysis is more difficult than consulting a crystal ball or a few smart analysts. In most real-world situations, the number of variables is large, time lines are long, the players are numerous and susceptible to pressures of many kinds, and everything is both dynamic and interactive. In a highly globalized and interdependent world, what happens anywhere can affect possibilities and developments everywhere. Because it is seldom practical to tackle the problem by building elaborate models that can be run on powerful computers to generate a comprehensive list of possible outcomes, the task has to be rendered manageable by making judgments about what factors or drivers are most important, where and when tipping points or thresholds exist, and whether and why developments seem to be moving along a different trajectory than had been anticipated. The exercise also involves identifying key institutions and individuals, who or what they heed when making decisions, and what they seek to accomplish, among other variables. The ultimate goal is to provide insights and signposts that will help U.S. decision makers to assess probabilities, set priorities, and develop strategies to shape outcomes.

I will now shift from a general and idealized discussion of strategic intelligence to three specific examples that illustrate the nature and utility of Intelligence Community efforts to inform decisions about the future. I will not address the use of covert methods to manipulate events.[9] The reason is not simply that I cannot address classified activities in an unclassified discussion. That is certainly the case, but a more important reason is that my own estimate of their impact is rather low. If one divides the impact of covert manipulation into three categories (decisive, marginal, and irrelevant), I believe most should be classified as of marginal or no relevance to what actually happened. Others will disagree with this assessment, but I do not intend to provide additional evidence or justification for my opinion except to note the requirement that if such activity played a key role in U.S. foreign policy, it must be noted in the legally mandated compilation of documents produced by the State Department in the series entitled "Foreign Relations of the United States."[10] The number of examples in that compilation is very small.

EXAMPLES OF PROJECTS INTENDED TO HELP OFFICIALS TO ANTICIPATE AND SHAPE THE FUTURE

The first illustrative example is a completely unclassified study entitled *Global Trends 2025: A Transformed World*.[11] Although I will mention a few of its findings, my focus here will be on purpose and process.[12]

Global Trends 2025 is the fourth iteration of an exercise that began in the mid-1990s under the leadership of John Gannon, one of my predecessors as chairman of the National Intelligence Council. I participated in that effort and launched a parallel study at the State Department. These initial efforts attempted to describe the world of 2010.[13] Our motivations were similar: to see if we could do it, to learn from the process, and to answer complaints that we did not do enough strategic analysis. The exercise proved to be both difficult and rewarding. It was difficult, in part, because analysts were very uncomfortable driving so far beyond the headlights. We had almost no intelligence on what was likely to happen fifteen years into the future, and the coping strategy for many analysts was to project continuation of then-current trends. Most analysts, and the studies we produced, attempted to predict what would happen, and they were not very good at identifying drivers and potential sources of discontinuity. Perhaps the most important lesson we learned from this exercise was that it changed for the better the way participating analysts thought about their subjects and the utility of strategic analysis for understanding current events.[14]

The second iteration was launched a few years later, but unlike the first attempt, which had relied entirely on Intelligence Community analysts, the effort to identify trends out to 2015 convened several meetings to tap the expertise and insights of U.S.-based specialists on issues that we thought would be important over the next fifteen years. The second effort was less predictive and made more effective use of scenarios to help analysts and readers to think about issues and relationships.[15]

By the time we prepared for the third iteration, in 2004, we had a much clearer idea about the target audience, what we wanted to accomplish, and how to achieve our objectives. We produced *Global Trends 2020* in December so that it would be available at the start of a new administration when officials would be thinking about what they wanted to accomplish over the next four years. We wanted to catch them before the tyranny of the in-box made it more difficult to foster consideration of how short-term decisions might affect long-term developments. This time, we expanded the universe of experts far beyond those in the United States. We convened more than two dozen seminars and workshops on five continents to elicit the views of foreign as well as American scholars, journalists, business leaders, and officials. Intelligence Community analysts drew on the insights from these sessions when drafting the final report.[16]

Publication of *Global Trends 2020*, and the way it was produced, had impacts far beyond what any of us had anticipated. We gained understanding and insight from our foreign contributors, but, as important, involving hundreds of non–U.S. citizens in the process gave them an interest in the product and an incentive to use it in their own countries. This edition was translated into several languages, was adopted in university courses around the globe, and became the starting point for longer-term policy deliberations in many countries besides our own. Other nations benefited from what we had learned, and many acknowledged that they could not have undertaken anything even remotely comparable on their own. Interestingly, however, many who encountered the *Global Trends* exercise for the first time interpreted it as a prediction of what the United States thought was going to happen or, even more strikingly, as what the United States wanted to happen over the next decade and a half. The latter interpretation is particularly striking because one of the scenarios envisions a Jihadist victory and establishment of a new caliphate in the Middle East.[17] How anyone could interpret that thought-provoking scenario as an outcome desired by Washington is hard for me to understand.

When a few of us sat down in late 2007 to determine what we wanted to accomplish and how we would produce the fourth iteration of *Global Trends*, we recognized that we had an unprecedented combination of opportunity, experience, and willing participants. We knew that the 2008 election would result in an almost complete changeover of senior officials, no matter who won, and we saw this as a rare opportunity to help senior policy makers build their agendas with awareness of longer-term trends. In my experience, the start of a new administration is one of the few times officials have the time and appetite for strategic thinking; we were determined to hit that window of opportunity. Moreover, we had learned from our *Global Trends 2020* experience that non-Americans had much to contribute and would be influenced by our next look to the future. This offered an opportunity for focused dialog with influential people from many nations on issues that they and the Americans who would produce *Global Trends 2025* considered to be among the most important. This, in turn, offered opportunities for collaboration to address those and other issues. The 2025 report has been translated into Chinese, Korean, and probably other languages, and my former NIC colleagues and I have given dozens of public presentations in the United States and around the world.[18]

We made one major procedural change in the way we prepared the 2025 report. This time, we invited both American and non-American contributors to comment on draft versions of the report. We solicited input through a variety of conferences, seminars, and commissioned studies, as we had done previously. But this time we also posted drafts on a special website and invited continuing interchange to ensure that we had understood points correctly, to smoke out alternative judgments, and to ensure that we were communicating judgments effectively.[19] The process worked. We produced a better product, and we built interest in and support for the project among influential people around the world.

Before commenting briefly on some of the report's findings, I want to flag two additional points with respect to process and purpose. First, *Global Trends 2025* does not predict what will happen. What it does do is describe a dozen or so trends that appear likely to drive, shape, and constrain the actions of individuals, firms, nations, and the international system as a whole. They are not the only trends that will be important, and it is certain that we did not get it completely right with respect to the factors we did examine. But, at a minimum, the trends and drivers we examined reflect what members of the foreign policy elites of many countries think is going to happen and are already beginning to factor into their own plans and policy options.[20] In certain respects, perceived reality may be more important than reality itself because many players will act on the "reality" we captured in *Global Trends 2025*. Some of the trends appear likely to spawn or fuel competition or conflict, but many others offer opportunities for cooperation and sufficient lead time for unilateral and coordinated action.

The second point is that *Global Trends 2025* does not offer a road map or recipe for addressing the developments cited. Our purpose was to tell officials what they should consider, not what they should do. The message, in effect, was, "Here are the trends that we judge will be important over the next fifteen years. If you like where they are headed, you should devise policies to preserve their projected trajectory. If you don't like where they are headed, you should begin now to consider ways to shift them in a more favorable direction. The ultimate success of the policy agendas you develop will be influenced by how that agenda intersects with the trends we have identified. What to do is up to you."

The decision to eschew policy recommendations was an easy one because professional ethics enjoin the Intelligence Community from policy advocacy. That certainly does not mean that individuals working on the report had no thoughts about whether or how to take advantage of or attempt to alter the trends we discovered. We did. I certainly did. In this case, as is true most of the time, I think we did a pretty good job of insulating the analysis of trends from personal attempts to spin them in particular ways. That said, I think those of us who were most deeply engaged in the project would have been disappointed if nobody asked for our thoughts on what might be done. I can assure you that when *Global Trends 2025* project director Mat Burrows and I briefed then President-elect Obama on our findings, we did not refuse to answer when he asked for our thoughts on what to do with respect to certain of the issues and trends discussed in the report.

Global Trends 2025, like its predecessors, was designed to stimulate discussion, debate, and strategic thinking about the future. Some have characterized it as a pessimistic prediction of U.S. decline and unstoppable erosion of the global institutions that have fostered peace and prosperity for more than half a century.[21] Others have focused on only one or a few of its findings.[22] Still others have underscored the report's judgment that the future is neither inevitable nor immutable.[23] The last time that I checked, a Google search for "Global Trends 2025" yielded almost 176,000 results. If nothing else, we did stimulate discussion. Discussion of the issues we addressed by persons outside of the U.S. government is a good thing, but our primary audience was, of course, the incoming administration and career officials in Washington. I can write with confidence that the report was read and discussed and that it continues to serve as a frame of reference for discussion and decisions.

As noted previously, the purpose of reports in the *Global Trends* series is to identify trends and drivers that appear likely to constrain and challenge decision makers around the world. The factors discussed in the report will not determine the future, but they will shape it by constraining (or expanding) options, commanding leadership attention and other finite resources, and creating conditions conducive to both conflict and cooperation. The factors exist and will help to shape our future, but their impact will be mediated by the decisions of political, economic, societal, and technical leaders. In other words, they will help set and shape the agendas of decision makers, but it will be the decisions, not the drivers themselves, that will have the greatest impact on the future course of events.[24] Key factors examined in the *Global Trends 2025* report are summarized below. Readers are reminded that they are trends and drivers that will shape the future, *not* predictions of what the future will be.

One of the long-evolving trends that we expect to continue involves the cluster of developments subsumed under the heading of globalization. We anticipate that globalization will continue, albeit possibly at a somewhat slower pace than before the economic downturn that began in 2008, and that it will continue to foster both unprecedented prosperity and growing inequality. More people will become wealthier, but the gap between rich and poor will widen.[25]

Developments linked to globalization, but having other dynamics and drivers as well, include the rise of Brazil, Russia, India, and China (the so-called BRICs) as well as a number of other nations. The report anticipates that the next "wave" of rising states will include Indonesia, Turkey, and, possibly, Iran.[26] The rise of new powers and the weaknesses in existing multilateral institutions illustrated by the global financial crisis underscore the decreasing efficacy of the post–WW II institutions that made possible globalization and the rise of the BRICs and others benefiting from the current international order. But that order—the United Nations, the World Bank and other multilateral financial institutions, alliances formed to deter or defeat a country that no longer exists (the Soviet Union), and numerous control regimes such as the Nuclear Non-proliferation Treaty—is showing its age. It was forged in a different time to manage a world very different from that of today.[27]

Those institutions, and the global order they make possible, are increasingly in need of reform, reengineering, or replacement. Remaking the global order will be much more difficult than it was in the 1940s. For starters, there are 140 more countries today, and norms of equality and democratic participation mean that most will demand a seat at the table. The United States remains the preeminent power, but the gap between the United States and the rest is narrowing. We are not in decline, and we benefit enormously from the rise of the rest, but we are no longer the undisputed leader of the "free world." The need for major changes to the global order is increasingly apparent, but key players who benefit from the status quo—the rising powers—are not eager to change it because any replacement order will require them to assume greater responsibility. Change is impossible without their active participation, but they have strong incentives to stretch out the current order—in which the United States serves as the ultimate guarantor of peace and prosperity and others can be free riders—for as long as possible.

I will close this section by mentioning without elaboration four additional trends. The first is demographic. Global population will grow by 1.2 billion between 2008 and 2025. Less than 3 percent of that growth will be in the West—the United States, Europe, Canada, and Australia, plus Japan and South Korea. The most developed nations will face major challenges associated with the graying of their populations; the rest of the world must deal with youth bulges. Much of the projected growth will occur in Africa, Central Asia, and Central America, where governments already struggle to meet expectations and requirements. Youth bulges will increase demand for education, jobs, and opportunity that probably cannot be satisfied by governments that are already struggling.[28] Add to this the initial impact of changes caused or exacerbated by global climate change, which scientists tell us will begin to be felt between 2025 and 2030. These effects will change weather patterns, exacerbate water shortages in some places and flooding in others, and stress food supplies in places already living close to subsistence levels.[29] On a happier note, the appeal of extremist ideologies will continue to decrease, as will the number of terrorists and terrorist groups. However, the potential lethality of terrorist attacks will increase because of advances in bioengineering that make use of lethal biological agents more likely.[30] Globalization-facilitated growth will increase the demand for energy and other resources, with likely increases in price and the potential for conflict to ensure access.[31] This will provide impetus to the search for greener technologies, but the transition to a system based on alternatives to hydrocarbons cannot be achieved in fifteen years.[32]

GEOPOLITICAL IMPLICATIONS
OF GLOBAL CLIMATE CHANGE

Global Trends 2025 was a self-initiated project. No one told us to do it, no one told us what to address, and no one pressed us to deliver our conclusions before we were ready. In these and other respects, it was truly unique (for example, in the positive reception it received from members of Congress on both sides of the aisle). The National Intelligence Assessment on the geopolitical implications of global climate change that we produced a few months earlier had a very different history and reception. I should note in passing that National Intelligence Assessment (or NIA) is one of those terms of art that is important to cognoscenti and almost meaningless to anyone else. The short explanation of the difference between an NIA and the better-known National Intelligence Estimate (or NIE) is that an NIA addresses subjects that are so far in the future or on which there is so little intelligence that they are more like extended think pieces than estimative analysis. NIAs rely more on carefully articulated assumptions than on established fact.

I should probably take it as a badge of achievement that members of Congress began to press for an NIE on global climate change in late 2006 and early 2007.[33] The reason I say this is that I made improvement in the quality of analysis, notably NIEs, and the restoration of confidence in the quality of IC analytic work my highest priorities when I became deputy director of national intelligence for analysis and chairman of the National Intelligence Council in mid-2005. By 2007, we had regained the confidence of a growing number of members who began to request NIEs to have reliable and objective assessments of important issues—or so they said. Many of these requests came from Democrats who may have had an additional motivation, that is, to use NIEs as a stick with which to pummel the administration. That is a tale for another essay; here

I want to focus on climate change. The short setup for the story I'm about to tell is that whether climate change is occurring, the extent to which it is caused by human activity, whether the United States was incurring too high a price for being out of step with its allies on the importance of combating global warming, and a host of other politically charged issues provided the backdrop for the initial requests that the NIC produce an NIE on climate change. Another factor was the release and reception of former Vice President Al Gore's book and documentary on global warming, *An Inconvenient Truth*.[34]

To tell the story, I will compress a number of conversations with several members and staff into a single and greatly simplified set of invented exchanges that accurately reflect the dialog:

> Member: We need an estimate on climate change.
>
> Me: We don't do climate change; talk to NOAA or the National Academy of Sciences.
>
> Member: But we trust you and know we will get an objective assessment.
>
> Me: Thank you, but the NIC doesn't know anything about climate science.
>
> Member: But we trust you, and the NIC does analyze geopolitical developments, right?
>
> Me: Yes, but we still don't have any expertise on climate change.
>
> Member: OK, then do an NIE on the geopolitics of global climate change.

She had me. Congress eventually ordered us to produce an estimate on the geopolitical implications of global climate change.[35] Our first step was to decide how to say something meaningful without disgracing ourselves by misconstruing the science or straying too far into the political minefield.

Despite the rather inauspicious origins, we rather quickly discovered that producing this NIA would be highly educational for those who worked on it and that it had the potential to stimulate thinking about future U.S. policies in numerous areas. My focus here, once again, will be on process and purpose rather than on the substance of the report. The NIA remains classified, but the substantive content except for the names of countries likely to encounter and be unable to cope with climate change–induced problems can be found in the unclassified Statement for the Record that I submitted to the Congress in June 2008.[36]

Our first challenge was to establish a scientific baseline. Unable to make an independent judgment on climate science, we began by asking climate science experts to provide a general assessment of which regions and countries are likely to be relatively hard hit by climate change between now and 2030. Lacking appropriate in-house expertise, we enlisted the help of specialists from the Joint Global Change Research Institute (JGCRI), a joint undertaking of the University of Maryland and the Department of Energy's Pacific Northwest Laboratory. To develop the scientific scene-setter we needed, JGCRI used the most recent report by the Intergovernmental Panel on Climate Change (IPCC) and subsequently published peer-reviewed material. We solicited comments on the scene-setter from the U.S. Climate Change Science Program. We took that as our starting point and asked, "If those projections are correct, what effects would they produce between now and 2030?" We chose 2030 as the endpoint because looking out further than that required too many assumptions about politics, economics, social cohesion, and other variables to permit confident judgments. In addition, scientists seem to agree that nothing could be done that would alter the effects of climate change between now and 2030. That die had already been cast.

The next challenge was to ask how effects projected at a global level would be felt in specific regions, countries, and subnational areas. We enlisted the assistance of Columbia University's Center for International Earth Science Information Network (CIESIN) to develop country-specific data on water scarcity, climate vulnerability, and sea level rise. Among other things, we discovered that working at national and subnational levels required more granular information—greater detail—than was available for many countries. We communicated this "intelligence gap" or information requirement to other USG organizations working on climate change. The deficiencies might be addressed, at least in part, by reworking existing data, but our assessment established the need to collect additional data if we are to develop appropriate responses.

Our objectives in this phase of the study were to identify which places, peoples, and political systems would be affected by climate change during the period under study, which would be affected first, which would be most severely affected, which had the largest or most impoverished populations at risk, and so forth. To make the task more manageable, we focused on water, food production, and changes in weather patterns. Data issues made the results of this phase somewhat problematic, but we determined that what we had was the best we were likely to have for some time. This was a familiar situation because the intelligence business always deals with ambiguous and spotty data; the key was to communicate effectively the uncertainties and limitations of our results.

After integrating the results from the independent studies to obtain a composite map of relative impacts from climate change, we set out to discover which of the places affected by climate change had sufficient economic, technical, and governmental resources to deal with the problem and which could be overwhelmed by the additional challenges. We then convened groups of country and area specialists and asked them to address a number of questions regarding the capability of governments and societies to cope with the challenges of climate change. This was obviously a subjective exercise, but we used multiple experts and integrated their judgments to produce a rough matrix of vulnerability. Only then did we ask questions about how climate change effects, government coping mechanisms, likely population movements to escape drought, and other factors might affect the United States and American interests.

The result was a pathbreaking study that identified areas for data collection, the need for new or refined analytic methodologies, and opportunities to begin dialog with officials to pave the way for collective action. We fed some of the results into the *Global Trends 2025* project, but we also brought them to the attention of a wide range of U.S. officials from the Department of Defense, the State Department, USAID, and other agencies so that they could begin developing strategies and plans to address the consequences we identified. Among the kinds of decisions we hoped to inform were: Should assistance be broadly distributed in the name of fairness or concentrated where it would do the most good? Should U.S. and/or coordinated efforts focus on the governments needing the most help (because they have severely limited capabilities) or on those most likely to use the assistance effectively? Should assistance efforts be focused on regions that will be affected first, on those with the most vulnerable populations, or on those with the greatest potential for spillover into other countries? The list of such questions can be extended quite easily, but the key point is that resources will be limited, the media will focus attention on specific situations, domestic constituencies in the United States will seek assistance for their homelands or coreligionists, and many other real-world factors will greatly complicate decision making on how to respond unless careful work is undertaken at an early date. We hoped that the NIA would stimulate that kind of strategic thinking.

The NIA on geopolitical implications of climate change has proven to be a useful and influential study, and I confess to being proud of our work. But you need to remember that the NIA was requested for mostly political reasons and was embroiled in controversy almost as soon as it was completed. The issue had nothing to do with its methodology or substantive findings; it was all about political gamesmanship. The first issue was classification. As attention to global warming increased as a result of Vice President Gore's book and documentary, calls for the Intelligence Community to produce an unclassified study increased. The request was not unreasonable; after all, almost none of the information used to produce it was classified. But use of classified information is not the only reason to restrict access to NIC or other USG products. I had two reasons for opposing declassification of this report. The first was the desire not to complicate diplomatic efforts to develop coping strategies by publishing the names of the countries, governments, and societies that we judged to be least capable of coping with the effects of climate change. I thought it best for American officials to develop a strategy to address the kinds of questions illustrated in the preceding paragraphs before being subjected to predictable additional pressures. I also wanted to avoid complicating negotiations on other matters by appearing to insult the capabilities of those with whom the United States was currently negotiating and involving places where American firms were pursuing investment and other forms of engagement. The second reason was that I did not want to fire the starting gun for the flight out of countries where we predicted impacts beyond the coping ability of their governments. To be blunt, I did not want to trigger an exodus before countries had a chance to devise strategies and mechanisms to keep people in or out of particular regions. Most of those with whom I discussed this on the Hill understood the logic but wanted to play a different game.

My offer—and the delivery—of unclassified testimony didn't solve the problem. It actually made it worse. Democrats and some Republicans wanted the report declassified to make the case for more urgent attention to the issues it identified. Republicans wanted it declassified to bolster their claim that Democrats had foolishly diverted intelligence resources to pursue a study that contained no intelligence and should have been undertaken by another agency.[37] I have to smile when I recall one memorable public exchange with a congressman who demanded to know why I had allowed the use of Intelligence Community resources to produce an NIE (he wasn't interested in the distinction I noted earlier) on climate change. I was delighted to be able to respond, "Because the Congress instructed me to do so."[38]

IRAN'S NUCLEAR INTENTIONS AND CAPABILITIES

I will close with one more short illustration of how intelligence can help officials to prepare for and shape the future. This example is drawn from the highly contentious 2007 National Intelligence Estimate on *Iran's Nuclear Intentions and Capabilities*. It became contentious, in part, because the White House instructed the Intelligence Community to release an unclassified version of the report's key judgments but declined to take responsibility for ordering its release.[39] Critics on the right and the left denounced or praised the report as a deliberate effort by the Intelligence Community—or, in many of the commentaries, by me—to derail administration plans to attack Iran.[40] This episode is examined in Chapter 6; what I want to do here is to take advantage of the fact that a small portion of the estimate was declassified (three of about 140 pages with none of the almost 1,500 source citations), making it possible for me to talk about it in public.[41]

Because this estimate is discussed in Chapters 5 and 6, I will focus here on just two of the findings intended to help policy makers to shape the future. One of the findings—actually a cluster of findings—attempts to answer the question, "How long until Iran has a nuclear weapon?" This is another way of addressing the question, "How long do we have to work this problem?" The prospect of an Iranian bomb and the deleterious consequences that would have for regional stability and global efforts to limit the spread of nuclear weapons had achieved high salience long before we prepared this estimate, but before answering these questions I will use this example to illustrate a broader point. In my experience, most policy makers ask themselves, and often ask their intelligence support team, whether the reported or projected development requires immediate action on their part or can be deferred while they work on more pressing issues or more attractive parts of their policy agendas. That is a natural and rational approach. To compensate for this, intelligence has a built-in, and on subjects like terrorism, a recently reinforced propensity to underscore, overstate, or "hype" the findings to get people to pay attention and to fireproof the IC against charges that it failed to provide adequate warning. I note in passing that this propensity was one of the reasons for the errors in the 2002 estimate on Iraq's weapons of mass destruction.[42]

The pacing element for production of a nuclear device or weapon is the acquisition of sufficient fissile material. The message of the estimate is clear: "You have some, but not a lot of, time." The key judgments state we had moderate to high confidence that Iran had not obtained sufficient fissile material from external sources and that its fastest route to having enough would be through uranium enrichment using centrifuges. The NIE said it was possible, but very unlikely, that Iran could do so as early as late 2009. We judged it more likely that it could do so "sometime during the 2010–2015 timeframe." The declassified portion of the estimate did not address how long it would take Iran to convert highly enriched uranium into a weapon, but the classified text did. What I can say here is that we judged Iran had the scientific, technical, and industrial capacity to produce a weapon if it decided to do so.

The second finding of direct relevance to this discussion is the judgment that Iran had halted the weaponization portions of its nuclear program in 2003 in response to international pressure and scrutiny. It interprets this development as indicative of a cost-benefit approach suggesting that diplomacy had been effective in 2003 and might still be an effective instrument for deterring Iran from acquiring a nuclear weapon. In other words, the message it was intended to send to policy makers was, "You do not have a lot of time, but you appear to have a diplomatic or nonmilitary option." Prior to the publication of this estimate, the judgment of the Intelligence Community—and of many pundits and policy makers—was that there was little to no chance of deterring Iran from pursuing a nuclear weapon and that only the use of force—military options—could prevent Tehran from acquiring the bomb. The estimate also judged, and stated clearly, that Iran at a minimum had retained the option to pursue a weapon and that whether to do so would be a political decision that could be made at any time.

How those judgments could be construed as dismissing the idea that Iranian nuclear activities were a major problem continues to mystify me, but the point I want to make here is that, in addition to many other things, the NIE gave policy makers a time line, a sense of urgency, and possible alternative ways to address the problem. We were helping them to anticipate and shape the future.

5 ESTIMATIVE ANALYSIS

What It Is, What It Isn't, and How to Read It

MUCH OF THE WORK of the Intelligence Community (IC) involves estimative analysis because many of the questions it is asked to address—and all of the important questions—have unknown or indeterminate answers. The best-known, most discussed, and most misunderstood form of estimative analysis is the National Intelligence Estimate (NIE). NIEs have been produced for more than sixty years, and many of the older ones have been declassified and published.[1] A few—in the grand scheme of things, very few—have become infamous for bad judgments and/or bad tradecraft, but most of them have been pretty good.[2] "Pretty good" should not be interpreted as disparaging their utility. Most were unexciting and unsurprising, and few scored theoretical breakthroughs. What they did do, most of the time, was to pull together the available evidence on issues important to decision makers, seek additional information to close "intelligence gaps," and interpret that evidence with the goal of characterizing the current situation as accurately as possible. They also ascertained where developments appeared to be headed and what would determine their speed and trajectory, and they explicated alternative possibilities, potential harbingers of change, and possible opportunities for U.S. policy makers to shape the course of events. Most of the time, they largely confirmed or validated what those working the issues already knew, or thought that they knew, about the subject.

That they did not present new discoveries or theoretical breakthroughs did not make them irrelevant or useless; to the contrary, a validating second opinion on matters that had risen to the top of the U.S. foreign policy agenda was—and still is—an important contribution to the decision-making process. Moreover, that NIEs contain no surprises for those working the issues is a sign that the process of intelligence support is working properly. Something would be very wrong if officials responsible for working an issue learned about new information germane to the issue or new interpretations of that information by reading an NIE. If their intelligence support team were doing its job, and the process were working as it should, new information and insights would have been factored into the decision-making process long before an NIE had been approved and published. Stated another way, NIEs are not and should not be the mechanism that alerts policy makers to new findings. Rather, they are a kind of "for the record" snapshot that captures the thinking of the Intelligence Community on a particular issue or set of issues. As explained in the following pages, the process whereby NIEs are produced is more important, in many respects, than is the product that results from the process.

The total readership of most NIEs is quite small, and most who do read them are not senior U.S. government policy makers. This is a point that has been made many times, often followed by a recommendation that they be abandoned as an art form.[3] I do not agree with that recommendation (see the following discussion), but the point I wish to make here is that estimative analysis, including but not limited to NIEs, may be less influential as stand-alone products than when it is used in the preparation of a number of influential and authoritative statements of administration and/or U.S. government views on important issues. One type of statement takes the form of "statements for the record" and the answers to "questions for the record" prepared in response to congressional requests. Many such products are prepared in unclassified as well as classified versions, and much of the time they are read and parsed much more closely than are the NIEs and other products used in their preparation. Other types of U.S. government statements informed by the judgments reflected in NIEs and other estimative products include speeches by executive branch officials that provide background information to explain or justify policy decisions and diplomatic demarches intended to inform and influence other nations. Such statements seldom make explicit reference to an estimative product, but most have been examined carefully to ensure that what they say is consistent with the findings of the Intelligence Community. Policy makers can, and occasionally do, articulate positions different from the judgments of the Intelligence Community. But, when the system works as it should, they do so knowing that the IC will articulate a different judgment if asked by a member of Congress or other executive branch officials.[4]

Perhaps the single most informative and, possibly, most influential estimative product is the Annual Threat Assessment submitted to several congressional oversight committees to inform hearings on the president's budget. Since 2006, the director of national intelligence has presented a single threat assessment (in both classified and unclassified versions) on behalf of the Intelligence Community as a whole.[5] In contrast to NIEs, Annual Threat Assessments are not formally "coordinated" or reviewed by the National Intelligence Board (see the following discussion), but they are subjected to rigorous review to revalidate or revise judgments presented in previously published assessments and to determine whether (and why) any agencies or analysts hold different views on the judgments being cited. Such statements for the record build on and incorporate the findings of previously produced NIEs and other estimative products. Knowing that every judgment in them is likely to be subjected to close scrutiny by members and staff to determine consistency with classified briefings and analytic products that have been provided to Congress previously, the IC analysts who prepare them, now under the direction of the chairman of the National Intelligence Council, take pains to explain any changes of judgment resulting from the review and reassessment of previously reached judgments that are now a normal part of the process. Congressional staff read the statements closely to prepare questions for administration witnesses and for information and insight that will help them evaluate administration policy decisions and legislative proposals. That, as one might anticipate, provides a strong incentive for executive branch officials to ensure that they understand what IC analysts have said to the Hill.

DRIVING BEYOND THE HEADLIGHTS

Estimates always and intentionally push beyond what is known—or believed— to be true. If we had all the facts, that is, if there were no intelligence gaps, there would be no need to close gaps with estimative judgments. If we "knew" what foreign decision makers would do under specified conditions, we would not have to assess or estimate how they would reach a decision and what they would decide. One of the most frequent, and most frustrating, mischaracterizations of estimative analyses, particularly NIEs, is a tendency to describe and evaluate them as if they were—or pretended to be—statements of fact or unqualified predictions. Former Acting Director of Central Intelligence John McLaughlin made this point very effectively in an appearance on CNN in which he said:

> National estimates are a widely misunderstood art form. When they become public, as this one [the 2007 NIE on Iran's nuclear intentions and capabilities] did, they are always heralded as the "most authoritative" documents the intelligence agencies produce. Perhaps because they so rarely appear in public, estimates are treated by critics and proponents alike as though what they say is chiseled in stone—"facts" that can be established like evidence in a courtroom trial. As the arguments rage, everyone seems to forget that these are not facts but judgments. In the best of cases, they are judgments based on a sizeable body of fact—seemingly the case in the latest Iran estimate—but the facts are never so complete as to remove all uncertainty from the judgment.[6]

Misunderstanding and misconstruing what NIEs are, what they attempt to do, and how they should be read are not limited to the media and politically motivated members of the punditocracy. It has been my experience that many "customers" of the Intelligence Community, including members of both the executive branch and the Congress, also have a misinformed or distorted view of estimative products and the purposes for which they are prepared. Regrettably, many IC analysts share at least some of the misconceptions.[7] What follows is an attempt to clarify the purpose and how to "read" estimative analysis and to correct some of the most common misconceptions.[8]

Confusion and misconceptions about what an NIE is (and is not) result, in part, from the way they are described in Intelligence Community publications. For example, the National Intelligence Council page on the director of national intelligence website describes NIEs as "the DNI's most authoritative written judgments concerning national security issues."[9] The same characterization appears at the beginning of the one-page description of NIEs and the NIE process that has been issued together with the declassified key judgments of a few recently produced estimates. The first paragraph of that description states:

> National Intelligence Estimates (NIEs) are the Intelligence Community's (IC) most authoritative written judgments on national security issues and designed to help US civilian and military leaders develop policies to protect US national security interests. NIEs usually provide information on the current state of play but are primarily "estimative"—that is, they make judgments about the likely course of future events and identify the implications for US policy.[10]

Those who report on or critique estimates usually emphasize, without explaining, their authoritativeness; virtually none note or explain that they are "primarily 'estimative.'"[11] The meaning of "most authoritative" conveyed by virtually all commentators implies that their findings are "definitive" or "the best" or even the "most accurate" assessments produced by the Intelligence Community. What it actually means is more prosaic, some might even say bureaucratic. Estimates are the "most authoritative" judgments of the Intelligence Community because they are issued in the name of the director of national intelligence (the director of central intelligence prior to the standup of the Office of the Director of National Intelligence in 2005). They are also considered authoritative because they have been approved by the National Intelligence Board (known previously as the National Foreign Intelligence Board), which is comprised of the heads of all analytic components of the IC.[12] In other words, what makes NIEs authoritative is the fact that they have been vetted and approved by the heads of all agencies and issued in the name of the senior official of the Intelligence Community. They do not represent the views of a single agency, component of an agency, or the formally or informally coordinated work of analysts in two or more constituent agencies. NIEs have gone to the top of the bureaucratic totem pole, and the heads of each agency have taken responsibility for the judgments and the tradecraft used to produce them. Agency heads take this responsibility very seriously, but doing so does not endow them with perfect understanding of complex situations or the ability to see into the future.

NIEs are not revealed truth or infallible prophecy. They are exactly what the name connotes—approximations informed by intelligence and the insights and expertise of analysts from across the Intelligence Community. They are unlikely ever to be as accurate as are estimates of settlement costs prepared as part of real estate transactions because, in the latter case, all but a few of the component costs are known with precision and will not change between the time of preparation and the time of closing. Estimates of construction costs and completion dates are notoriously problematic even though those who prepare them do not have to contend with deception, unknown intentions, and other challenges encountered routinely in intelligence analysis.[13] Stated another way, NIEs are not and should not pretend to be more than approximations or projections of developments that cannot be measured with precision, interact in unknown or uncertain ways, and could evolve in quite different ways depending on decisions made by people subject to a variety of personal, political, and other influences.

The primary purpose of most intelligence estimates is, or should be, to enhance decision maker understanding of complex and potentially consequential issues shrouded in mystery, secrets, and enigmas. The goal is to help them to anticipate, abet, alter, avoid, or ameliorate developments that they find desirable, dangerous, or disruptive. This requires doing more than rehearsing known facts and itemizing what we do not know about a situation. Most decision makers working on the problem probably already know that. What they want, need, and expect is a rigorous effort by the Intelligence Community to close information gaps through stepped-up collection and/or the clear articulation of assumptions about capabilities, priorities, and other unknowns. Estimates should give them a clearer picture of the possibility space within which events are likely to play out, what is likely to drive or deflect developments from the trajectories they seem to be on, and what might signal that change is occurring with respect to one or more drivers or trajectories. Estimates should also provide insight that will help decision makers to determine what they can do about projected developments and how long they have to work the problem.

Estimates always involve uncertainty—if they did not, they would not be "estimates"—but how uncertainties are handled often is shaped or determined by the purpose for which the estimate has been undertaken. For example, if asked to estimate the military capabilities of an adversary, there is a natural and prudent tendency to err in the direction of overestimation or "worst-case" judgments because preparations made to meet worst-case possibilities almost automatically ensure that lesser capabilities can be defeated. Erring in the other direction, that is, underestimating the adversary's capabilities, could lead to disaster on the battlefield. In general, it is prudent to overestimate the capabilities of a potential adversary and to prepare accordingly, but this general rule works better for military assessments than for others. Indeed, when applied to nonmilitary issues, worst-case analysis can be unhelpful or counterproductive. A better approach, most of the time, is to bound the range of the possible with best-case and worst-case judgments that frame estimates of more likely possibilities. Two examples illustrate this point.

In the early 1990s, IC analysts were sharply divided on the question of whether North Korea was implacably committed to acquiring nuclear weapons or might be willing to negotiate away its nuclear program in exchange for recognition and security assurances from the United States that would alleviate Pyongyang's security concerns and open the way to greater prosperity through international engagement. Analysts on one side (and all agencies except the State Department's Bureau of Intelligence and Research) interpreted ambiguous evidence in a "prudently" worst-case way and concluded that Pyongyang was determined to acquire nuclear weapons, would not negotiate in good faith, and would not agree to abandon its nuclear program. The implication of this analysis was that Clinton administration officials could not secure a halt to the North's program through negotiations and would have to find other means to address the problem.

Those on the other side (mainly but not exclusively in INR) argued that the North *might* be willing to negotiate away its nuclear program and that the best way to find out if that were the case would be to sit down at the negotiating table. The administration decided to attempt negotiations and was severely criticized by members of Congress for foolishly embarking on a feckless adventure that could not succeed.[14] The atmosphere on the Hill improved slightly, for a time, after then Chairman of the National Intelligence Council Joe Nye laid out for members the alternative judgments of IC analysts. For reasons having to do with the way intelligence was made available to members at the time, few—if any—were aware of the "might be willing to negotiate" judgment. After Nye laid out the alternative judgments, Senator Sam Nunn of Georgia stated that he was now able to understand why the administration was willing to negotiate and that in the past he had found it impossible to reconcile White House actions with the only IC judgment that he had seen because that assessment judged that negotiations could not achieve the desired outcome. I suspect a fair amount of political gamesmanship in this statement (given his previous support for negotiations), but the point he made, namely that it is difficult to defend policy decisions that seem inconsistent with intelligence judgments, is an important one. Perhaps more to the point, these negotiations led to the "agreed framework" that halted the production of plutonium for the North Korean weapons program for eight years.

The second example is drawn from the 2002 NIE on Iraq's weapons of mass destruction (examined at greater length in Chapter 6). In retrospect, it is clear that the IC consistently adopted, albeit unconsciously, worst-case interpretations of partial and ambiguous intelligence on Saddam's chemical and biological weapons capabilities. Although the question to be examined was defined in a straightforward and seemingly unbiased fashion ("What do we know about Saddam's WMD capabilities and intentions?"), the context in which it was asked effectively transformed the question into one about military capabilities. The fact that the United States was clearly preparing for the possibility of military action against Iraq may have, and probably did, make analysts reluctant to state or imply that there was little to no chance that Saddam had produced chemical weapons (CW) and/or biological weapons (BW). Unless the probability was zero, our troops had to prepare for their possible use. The existence of intelligence reporting and knowledge of past capabilities and employment of chemical weapons against the Kurds and the Iranians made it impossible to argue that there was no possibility that U.S. or coalition troops would be attacked with CW or BW munitions.[15] Laying out the evidence that we possessed at the time, key portions of which we now know to have been fabricated, implied that we knew more than we did and was construed to mean that chemical and/or biological weapons would be found after Saddam's forces had been defeated.

An NIE is not a prediction. To argue that something *could* happen is not the same as a prediction that it *will* happen. Explication of the circumstances under which something might—or probably would not—occur, and what policy makers should look for to determine whether a particular development is becoming more or less likely is often more helpful than either a single path projection of the "this will happen" or "that horse will win the third race" variety or a listing of possible outcomes with no indication what will determine whether one or another of them actually occurs. Attempting to cover all possibilities is seldom very helpful because those who receive intelligence support already understand that the situation is complex and could play out in numerous ways. They want signposts that will help them to determine the direction and speed of movement and whether the trajectory is changing. Most of the time, analysts and those they support share the same basic assessment of current trajectories because they have access to the same information and have discussed alternative ways of interpreting that information. This is the way the system is supposed to work. Policy makers working on a given issue or cluster of issues do not need an NIE to give them the baseline scenario, but officials who have tangential responsibilities might find it helpful to have that scenario described in an NIE or similar assessment. Again, the key is to help them to decide whether anything is changing and, if so, why and what they might do to reinforce, stall, or deflect the change.

Most NIEs involve multivariant analysis with uneven amounts known about each variable and, often, lack of clarity about which variables are most important. This makes NIEs very different from most academic studies, which use historical data and known outcomes to explain which variables were most important in particular circumstances. In that sense, NIEs do not have the scientific rigor of many academic papers, but there is a fundamental difference between explaining why a known outcome has occurred and what might occur under partially or largely unknown conditions. Part of the estimative art involves judgment about what conditions are most likely to arise, how one would recognize that they had, and informed speculation about what might happen next. Bounding the possibility space by relegating most possible developments to the "unlikely" bin, albeit while devoting some attention to wild-card and "low probability/high impact" possibilities, is an important part of the estimative process. Good tradecraft requires rigorous consideration of a wide range of alternative possibilities before narrowing the range to a manageable number.

Estimates are intended to help decision makers to manage a problem or capitalize on an opportunity. A prediction that, in effect, posits an outcome as inevitable and therefore beyond the ability of policy makers to change is seldom very helpful because the key question most decision makers have is "What can I do about this?" or "What can I do to abet, ameliorate, or avoid a particular outcome?" Those who read NIEs as if they were predictions and score the performance of the IC by determining which calls were "right" and which were "wrong" miss the point if they do not also look at what the estimate did (or did not) say about factors driving events, what might deflect them onto a different trajectory, and what might be done to ensure continuation of positive trends. Sometimes, or in some ways, the most valuable estimates are those that help—or force—customers to appreciate the complexity of an issue and how little is known about it. In the case of estimates written several years in the past, it is also appropriate to examine U.S. policy initiatives germane to the issues examined in NIEs and other estimative products to determine whether they explicitly or implicitly seek to alter the course of events in ways consistent with the analysis of the Intelligence Community and, where events played out differently than "predicted," whether the reason might be attributable, in part, to U.S. diplomacy or other forms of government intervention.

TYPES OF ESTIMATES

National Intelligence Estimates and other forms of estimative analysis generally fall into one of two categories, short term (six to twenty-four months) and mid- to long term (twenty-four months or longer). The further into the future analysts attempt to look, the less information they have to work with and the lower the fidelity of their analysis and reliability of their judgments. That does not automatically make longer-term assessments less useful than short-term analyses, but it does require clear understanding of their limitations. Both categories of estimative analysis can and should have a strategic dimension and be more than a compilation of known "facts" and available intelligence. To be useful, NIEs must attempt to put currently available information into a strategic framework that explains the genesis of current developments and what will shape their evolutionary trajectory. Some estimates do this better than others, primarily, in my view, because they resist the temptation to flaunt what collectors have been able to obtain and to shy away from making calls that go beyond what can be ascribed to an intercept, an image, or the assertions of a traitor willing to give or sell information to an intelligence service.

Short-Term Assessments

Short-term assessments should look at trends, what is driving them, and at the objectives, policies, and tactics of decision makers in the country, nonstate actor, or other entity being studied. Such assessments can be either broad brush, that is, address where events are headed and why, or narrowly focused (for example, on the likelihood that a fragile coalition government will hold together during the period of the estimate or on what a new (non-U.S.) administration is likely to attempt during its first months in office. Generally speaking, the tighter the focus, the more useful the NIE. Assessments that are "all over the map" seldom provide useful insights that decision makers can use to calibrate and tailor U.S. policy initiatives to achieve U.S. objectives. For example, judgments about the durability and intentions of a fragile coalition government can help U.S. policy makers to decide whether to expend diplomatic capital to press for a particular course of action before the coalition falls or to wait until the coalition is replaced or something happens to prolong its tenure. A case in point involved the coalition that took power in Pakistan following the February 2008 election. It was an uneasy and in many ways unnatural alliance of traditional rivals the Pakistan Peoples Party and the Pakistan Muslim League (N).[16] Both the Bush and the Obama administrations had to decide whether and how hard to press the fragile coalition to take action against the Taliban and other insurgent groups operating along the Afghanistan–Pakistan border.[17]

Short-term analysis can also be narrowly focused on a single question or set of questions. An example of this type of estimate is the January 2007 NIE entitled "Prospects for Iraq's Stability: A Challenging Road Ahead." The esti-

mate focused on relationships among stability/security, political reconciliation, and economic reconstruction and concluded that enhanced security was
an essential prerequisite for both political reconciliation and reconstruction.
It also judged that the overall security situation would continue to deterio-
rate unless there was measurable progress during the next twelve to eighteen
months to reverse the growing polarization of society, the persistent weakness
of the security forces and the state in general, and all sides' recourse to violence.[18] The analysis that was summarized in this NIE was developed prior to
and during the review of policy that led to the so-called surge later in the year.
The estimate was published after the decision to change tactics had been made
and was therefore criticized by some as irrelevant to the decision-making
process. Such criticism willfully or uncomprehendingly misses the point that
it was the close and continual interchange between IC analysts and decision
makers during the policy review that led to the surge that was important, not
the "for the record" write up of the analysis embodied in the estimate itself.
A follow-on assessment, in the form of an update to the February 2007 NIE,
examined the impact of the surge on the security situation and again assessed
prospects for stability and political reconciliation. That assessment is entitled
"Prospects for Iraq's Stability: Some Security Progress but Political Reconciliation Elusive."[19]

A third variant of short-term estimative analysis attempts to answer the
question, "What is going on here?"; it has much in common with what is often
derisively referred to as "current intelligence." The difference between current intelligence and short-term estimative analysis is often in the eye of the
beholder. The distinction that I make is to regard as current intelligence any
analytic product that reports newly obtained information, usually in the form
of a gist with a brief comment indicating whether it is consistent or inconsistent with previous intelligence on the subject and indicating when and how
it was obtained (usually in very general terms). The implicit message being
conveyed with the information is, "We just got this, we do not yet know what
it means—or even if it is accurate—but we thought you should know about it."
The primary reasons for providing reports of this kind is to build rapport with
customers by alerting them to something that might be raised by one of their
colleagues, to forewarn them that analysts are examining new intelligence
that might cause them to revise their assessment of issues within the purview
of the customer, and to dissuade policy makers from going off half-cocked in
response to a report that may be less conclusive or less important than it appears to be on first reading.

According to my distinction, short-term estimative analysis provides a more considered assessment of new developments and/or newly obtained intelligence and attempts to answer questions of the "What is going on here?" "What does it mean?" "What has caused this?" and "What should we expect next?" variety. Journalists make a similar distinction when they provide a more considered and in-depth analysis of a development that is first reported with little commentary. For example, intelligence analysts informed USG policy makers as soon as they learned about efforts by Venezuelan President Hugo Chavez to expand his country's relationship with China but soon followed up with an assessment of what Chavez was attempting to do, why he was spinning developments as he did, and how the Chinese had responded to Venezuelan overtures.[20]

Mid- to Long-Range Strategic Estimates

Like other forms of estimative analysis, mid- to long-range estimates attempt to lay out where events are headed, what is driving them, what might cause them to move in a different direction, and how we might detect that a change had occurred. They should also indicate to policy makers how long they have to work the issue before an important threshold is crossed and identify potential opportunities to influence the course of events. A judgment that says, in effect, that events are moving inexorably in a particular direction and that there is nothing U.S. officials can do to alter the projected outcome does not give policy makers many options beyond preparing for the worst and attempting to demonstrate that they did everything possible in a failed attempt to prevent the inevitable from happening. In my experience, estimates seldom tell policy makers, in effect, that there is nothing they can do to change the situation. Even the May 2005 update assessment of Iran's nuclear program did not foreclose the possibility of dissuading Tehran from acquiring a nuclear weapon. It said,

> We assess with high confidence that Iran *currently* is determined to develop nuclear weapons despite its international obligations and international pressure, but *we do not assess that Iran is immovable* [emphasis added].[21]

The language used is a bit awkward but was intended to, and does, convey the judgment that Iran might be persuaded to abandon its pursuit of nuclear weapons. The controversial 2007 NIE on Iran's nuclear intentions and capabilities reached a slightly different judgment on the basis of newly acquired intelligence. That judgment was:

We judge with high confidence that in fall 2003 Tehran halted its nuclear weapons program. Judge with high confidence that the halt lasted at least several years . . . Assess with moderate confidence Tehran had not restarted its nuclear weapons program as of mid-2007, but *we do not know whether it currently intends to develop nuclear weapons*. Judge with high confidence that the halt was directed primarily in response to increasing international scrutiny and pressure resulting from exposure of Iran's previously undeclared nuclear work. Assess with moderate to high confidence that *Tehran at a minimum is keeping open the option to develop nuclear weapons* [emphasis added].[22]

The 2007 estimate provides more guidance on how to influence thinking in Tehran than does the 2005 update, but it also indicates that the clock is ticking and that Iran could, if it decided to do so, produce enough highly enriched uranium (HEU) for a weapon by late 2009 or, more likely, sometime during the 2010–2015 time frame. This is the same time frame specified in the 2005 update. Media and congressional attention focused on—and was derisive if not dismissive of—the judgment that Iran had halted weaponization components of its nuclear program (ignoring the alternative judgment of the Department of Energy and the National Intelligence Council stating that they had only moderate confidence that the halt to the specified activities represents a halt to Iran's entire nuclear weapons program) and largely ignored the judgments that diplomacy and pressure appear to have worked in the past and that the window of opportunity to stop the program before Iran acquired sufficient HEU for a weapon would close in as little as two years. These, in my view, were the most important judgments in the NIE because they said, in effect, diplomacy and pressure worked and might work again because Iran appears to apply cost-benefit analysis in its security calculus, but time to work the problem was diminishing rapidly.

Mid- to long-range estimates can also look backward in an effort to determine why a subsequently discovered development had occurred and establish a basis for assessing and anticipating what happens thereafter. An example of such backward-looking estimative analysis was a quickly but capably produced assessment that attempted to explain why Saudi Arabia had sought and China had provided nuclear-capable intermediate range ballistic missiles.[23] Failure to discover the sale and transfer of CSS-2 missiles until very late in the process has not been included in the normal litany of "intelligence failures," but in my view it deserves to be on the list because earlier detection might have made it possible to prevent the transfer. Be that as it may, when it was discovered, it became immediately imperative to discover or assess why it happened because without knowing why it would be much harder to devise a U.S. response that preserved the relationship with our long-term partners and de facto allies in Saudi Arabia, minimized damage to the still-fragile relationship with China, and avoided an arms race in the Middle East.

Strategic analysis must go beyond interpretation of the latest intelligence reporting and must involve more than straight-line extrapolation of past behavior or reporting. Most of the time, the future is like the past, with certain variations, and most of the time it is "safe" to predict basic continuity. Policy makers do not need intelligence or analysis to tell them that most trends continue on more or less the same trajectory. Indeed, basic continuity should normally be treated as a baseline condition. The interesting and important contributions of intelligence and analysis are those that indicate when, why, and how the trajectory might change.

GENESIS OF NIES AND FORMULATION OF KEY QUESTIONS

In theory, and ideally, requests for NIEs originate with policy makers. Most policy maker requests come from members of the executive branch but, in recent years, an unprecedented number have been requested—or mandated—by members of Congress.[24] Often, however, NIE topics are suggested by National Intelligence Officers (NIOs) or IC leaders who want a rigorous review of old intelligence and previously reached judgments in light of newly obtained information because they have become uncomfortable with the answers they must give to the question, "How long has it been since the last NIE on this subject?" or wish to use the NIE process to facilitate IC contributions to policy reviews on complex and/or high-profile issues. Ideally, estimates are undertaken to inform specific policy decisions, but in the real world decision makers seldom know or communicate their long-range intelligence needs with sufficient lead time to prepare an NIE. Most of the time, their requests for "coordinated" analytic products are satisfied by preparing shorter, less formal products such as "sense of the community" memoranda, and Intelligence Community briefs.

Although it is generally quite easy to obtain policy maker endorsement for the preparation of an estimate suggested by the IC, proposing certain topics can be a tricky proposition. IC analysts have a responsibility to monitor the impact and implications of USG actions and to report their findings to policy makers, but initiating an NIE on a high-profile policy undertaking can look like IC criticism of or attempts to change policy. Paul Pillar experienced this dilemma when, as NIO for the Near East and South Asia, he knew that it was important to identify and assess the likely consequences of a U.S.-led effort to overthrow Saddam but was understandably reluctant to initiate such an effort lest he—and the IC—be accused of second-guessing the decision to go to war.[25]

However the process is initiated, the next step is to clarify what policy makers want or need to know about the subject. There is little point in addressing subjects they are not interested in or think they already know well—unless the IC has reason to believe that decision makers have an incorrect understanding of key dynamics and their implications. This normally is accomplished through a combination of NIO conversations with senior policy makers working the issues and consultations between the NIO and senior analysts in a position to reflect the wants and needs of their principal customers. These conversations should, and usually do, define and bound the subject of the estimate.

The next step is to formulate questions—with one key question—that, if examined and answered, promise to provide useful insight on the issues of greatest interest to policy makers. This entails discussion and debate to illuminate "what we need to know to answer the core question." That discussion should not take the form of asking, "What questions do I know I can answer?" or "What questions will allow me to show off particular pieces of intelligence?" Avoiding these pitfalls is sometimes harder than it should be, probably because some analysts do not fully understand the purpose of an estimate.

Formulating key questions is best done collaboratively through an NIO-led discussion with analysts most knowledgeable about the subject. The same discussion/process should tease out a list of sources analysts think most germane to the subject and preliminary thoughts on what the available evidence suggests. It should also identify questions that it is important to answer but on which there is little or no intelligence and must therefore be addressed through a two-pronged strategy that tasks collectors to see what they can come up with on the subject within a specified (usually short) time and generates assumptions to close information gaps that cannot be closed in other ways.

The discussion should seek to identify or generate multiple assumptions for each intelligence gap. As a practical matter, it often turns out that analysts working the general problem have already begun to employ working hypotheses and assumptions, which should be articulated and explained to their peers. Ideally, preparation of the NIE should entail exploration of multiple competing hypotheses and alternative assumptions for as long as they appear consistent with known facts. This iterative process should eventually yield one (or, at most, two) key questions and a number of prior questions that must be answered before it will be possible to address the key question. This cascade of questions should both structure the analysis—shaping the outline for the estimate—and determine what is to be addressed in the key judgments of the estimate. Describing the process in this way makes it sound more mechanistic than it is or should be. It is almost always the case that work on an estimate generates additional questions and/or insights worthy of incorporation into the key judgments, and the temptation is strong to include them, but the threshold for treating judgments as central rather than peripheral should be high or the estimate will lose focus and the likelihood will increase that readers will "miss" what analysts consider the main point.

ADDRESSING KEY QUESTIONS

Specifying the key questions to be addressed defines the scope and focus of the estimate, but that is only the first step in a multistage process designed to produce a genuinely fresh look at old and new evidence, previous judgments, and alternative assumptions and hypotheses. In other words, no matter how many times or how recently the IC has examined the issues to be addressed in an estimate, the process mandates going back to basics and starting with a clean sheet of paper. That is what is supposed to happen, and to a large extent it does. Even though the subjects addressed by all estimates have been examined—and written on—by analysts in one or (usually) more elements of the IC, and both analysts and agencies may well have adopted or endorsed positions on one or more of the questions to be examined, the preparation of an estimate requires, to the extent possible, a zero-based analysis of both previous analytic judgments and the intelligence used to support them. This means going back to square one in some very specific ways. Previous judgments, especially if they are deemed germane to answering the central question or any of the prior questions to be addressed in the estimate, must be examined de novo; no judgment can be assumed to be still valid and simply carried forward as the starting point for subsequent analysis. This was one of the clearest and most important lessons learned by the analytic community and others who examined the flawed Iraq WMD estimate.[26]

This zero-based review must examine whether new information has been obtained since the judgment was reached and how the new information fits with previously obtained information (for example, is it consistent or inconsistent; does it seem to corroborate, disconfirm, or raise questions about the older information; does new information make it necessary to replace or revise assumptions; do alternative hypotheses now appear more or less plausible; and so on). Analysts must go through a similar zero-based review. The purpose of the review is to take a fresh look at the evidence without regard to what has been concluded previously. This is sometimes difficult to do because at least some of the analysts working on any given estimate will have looked at the evidence previously and reached conclusions about what it means. For many, there is an unconscious tendency to want the reexamination to validate the conclusions they had reached in an earlier look at the subject.

While analysts are revisiting previous judgments, collectors must rescrub the intelligence germane to the new estimate. This begins with a revetting of the reporting used to support previous judgments as well as reexamining reporting that analysts indicate they consider important to the new assessment. This, too, reflects lessons learned or relearned from the Iraq WMD estimate. Collectors—via a formal letter signed by the head of the agency or designee—must attest to the validity of the sources used in the estimate. George Tenet initiated this requirement, and its application was expanded by the ODNI. The process is time consuming but critical and has become a routine part of the NIE process.

One of the most common characterizations of NIEs describes them as the "consensus view of all U.S. intelligence agencies."[27] NIEs should seek clarity, not consensus. This was not always the case; for many years, the process did drive toward consensus and, inevitably, lowest common denominator judgments. The right of agency representatives to take "footnotes" (the term of art for dissenting opinions) was sacrosanct, but agencies other than INR very seldom articulated alternative judgments, and when INR did so—which was frequently—the process constrained length and construed narrowly the scope for disagreement. Overstating the situation, but not by much, an agency could state that it disagreed with a judgment but had only limited scope for explaining why or for challenging the premise, methodology, or evidence undergirding the consensus judgment.

The current process, which I readily admit was influenced as much by years of frustration with the previous way of handling alternative judgments as it was by lessons learned from the unhappy experience of the Iraq WMD estimate, is designed to smoke out analytic differences as soon as possible and to ensure that the reasons for the different judgments are fully explicated. Doing this early can identify sources that may not have been discovered or fully considered by analysts in other agencies, explicate assumptions used to close intelligence gaps, make clear when and why analysts accord different significance to particular reports, and so on. Early and fully transparent discussion of analytic disagreements resolves most of them, often by moving all analysts to a place different from where any of them had been initially. Ideally, analysts will have left their previous—and therefore "preliminary"— judgments outside the door so they can look at the information with fresh eyes. That obviously does not always happen, but it is the new norm or standard. Moreover, if, at the end of the process, analysts continue to reach different judgments after considering the same information, that fact is as important to convey to policy makers as are the contending judgments themselves. Simply stated, if smart analysts with access to the same information come to different conclusions after thorough vetting of the intelligence and transparent discussion of how they reached their judgments, neither they nor policy makers can have high confidence in either/any of the contested judgments. Conveying the warning that the ice under judgments is thin is or can be even more important than the judgments themselves.

NIEs are not and should not be produced in a vacuum; the policy makers who requested the estimate and others known to be working on the issues examined should be continuously updated on main lines of analysis, preliminary findings, and any new intelligence germane to the project. If this triggers additional questions from policy makers, the questions should be addressed. Analysts complain about having to do so, but the purpose of intelligence is to inform and support decision makers, not to make life easy for analysts. Often the status updates lead to requests for formal briefings and/or analyst participation in a meeting of the Principals' Committee (PC), Deputies' Committee (DC), or other policy deliberation (as happened when preparing estimates on Iraq, Afghanistan, and a host of other subjects). The "process" must be capable of making useful input into the deliberative process at any time. Usually this would be done by the NIO or deputy NIO honchoing the effort, but the task might also be assigned to one of the lead drafters. Whoever attends for the IC must make clear the status of judgments at the time; they remain preliminary until they are considered and approved by the National Intelligence Board and the DNI. Prior to that, the estimate is a work in progress.

HOW TO READ AN ESTIMATE

One of the most asserted and misleading laments about estimates is that "nobody" reads them, or "no policy maker ever reads them." Such critiques often go on to say that no busy policy maker has time to wade through excessively long documents that tell little that he or she did not already know. I believe the observation to be basically correct but disagree strongly with the implication—or sometimes-explicit recommendation—that the production of NIEs is a waste of time that should be discontinued.

The reason "most" policy makers do not read NIEs is that most policy makers do not work the issues addressed in any particular NIE. No matter how short, how well written, how insightful, or how useful to those actually working the issues addressed, an estimate on India or Ukraine will not be read by policy makers responsible for Latin America or the Middle East unless they are informed that a specific portion of the estimate addresses an issue they are working, in which case they will read the relevant paragraphs. Why would anyone expect them to do otherwise?

The converse explains why many of those who do work the issues covered by a particular estimate do not bother to read it; if their intelligence support team has done its job, they already know what it says long before the NIE is published. Decision makers, almost by definition, are busy people who are not going to devote much time to reading classified products (which they can do only in designated areas that usually take them out of their offices) to learn what they already know.

If "nobody" (which really means no or very few senior policy makers) reads estimates, why bother to produce them? And what is the meaning of declaring NIEs to be the most authoritative analytic judgments of the Intelligence Community? The answer, or at least my answer, is that there are other reasons and audiences.

The first reason for going to the effort to produce an NIE is to clarify analytic thinking on important issues. Absent the production of an NIE or one of the other formally "coordinated" products produced by the NIC, analysts in different agencies (or even within the same big agency) would work with less knowledge of the thinking of colleagues elsewhere in the IC, might be working without knowledge of particular reports or streams of reporting, might be unaware of alternative hypotheses and assumptions, and might not know—or be able to inform their own policy customers—what counterparts elsewhere in the executive branch are being told by their own intelligence support teams.

In other words, producing an estimate forces collaboration and information sharing on the most important issues being worked in the national security establishment. This has pedagogic as well as demonstration value and helps elevate the quality of work done not only by the analysts who participate in the preparation of the NIE but also by others with whom they come in contact. Moreover, because the heads of agencies sitting as the National Intelligence Board must approve NIEs, they must become personally engaged in the process. This means that subordinates must also become engaged—to evaluate and explain the estimate to those above them in the bureaucratic food chain and to provide guidance to "their" representatives attending the coordination process. In short, there are many spillover and secondary effects that are good for the analytic process and for the integration of work done by the IC.

The second reason is that NIEs are read by many people below the level of senior policy makers. Desk officers, foreign service officers, and defense attachés preparing for new assignments; analysts picking up new accounts; persons newly assigned to the National Security Council; and others read them to come up to speed on key issues in key places. This is a very important audience because persons at this level are the ones who draft background papers, prepare talking points and congressional testimony, and formulate policy options to be considered by those higher in the bureaucracy. The quality of the decisions that emerge at the top of the system is influenced, if not determined, by the quality of the input made by subordinate officials. It is therefore at least as important that they be aware of the "best" thinking of intelligence analysts as it is that seniormost officials know what analysts think about their issues.

Foreign partners are another important audience for NIEs. Our liaison and diplomatic partners look to and rely on the United States for analysis of issues and regions that they do not cover in depth and/or because it helps them to understand U.S. foreign policy if they know the analytic thinking that undergirds the policy. Few estimates are shared in their entirety, but redacted versions, classified summaries of key judgments, and briefings on process as well as judgments can be very helpful to our partners and, more importantly, to the ability of U.S. officials to enlist foreign support on matters of importance to the United States. Estimates are far more than just "trading material" that can be exchanged for (usually much smaller amounts of) information and analysis prepared independently by counterparts with different sources of information and different policy customers. It is gratifying and a bit daunting to be thanked as profusely as I have been by foreign counterparts for whom our estimative products are an irreplaceable source of information and insight for their governments. Indeed, during my years in the State Department, senior officials in three allied governments told me on different occasions that the assessments provided to them on major portions of the world were regularly repackaged for their own more senior officials with little or no commentary beyond noting that they had been prepared by the U.S. Intelligence Community.

WHAT TO LOOK FOR IN AN NIE

During the past decade, NIEs have been used as cudgels with which to pummel political opponents or administration policies more frequently than at any previous time in my career. This has added another layer of challenge to their preparation because one now must try to anticipate not only whether anything has been written ambiguously and could be misinterpreted but also whether anyone will seize upon a particular word, phrase, or judgment to attack a policy or political opponent. Avoiding politicization during the preparation of an estimate is, in my experience, very easy to do because policy makers are almost always smart enough not to risk calumny by attempting to sway or skew analytic judgments and because analysts are extremely sensitive about interference with their tradecraft and spring loaded to resist any attempt to politicize their judgments. This admittedly impressionistic judgment is supported by the findings of the intelligence reform legislation–mandated annual survey that asks analysts if they have experienced or heard about instances of attempted politicization. The results have been basically the same every year; the number of instances reported is very small, and in virtually every case the attempt is reported to have been rebuffed by the analyst or agency involved. Politicization after publication is another matter, however, and avoiding the use of estimative judgments—and estimates themselves—for political purposes is almost impossible.

NIEs are authoritative, but they are not predictive or definitive. What makes them authoritative is that they have been approved by the heads of all analytic agencies, and the heads of collection activities have attested to the quality of the intelligence used to support judgments in the estimates. This also affirms that the way the intelligence has been used is consistent with the reporting (in other words, that the analysts have not misused the reporting). They distinguish between facts that can be confirmed (transparency into methodology and "showing of homework" makes this possible for those who want to check our tradecraft), "facts" that have been claimed or reported but cannot be independently confirmed, assumptions used to close information gaps, and analytic judgments. Judgments are not facts; they are the considered assessments of experienced analysts working with imperfect information.

NIEs (and other analytic products) should convey confidence judgments whenever it is appropriate to do so. Confidence judgments are based on the quantity, quality, and consistency of the information available to inform that judgment and judgments about the plausibility of alternative explanations or hypotheses. High confidence does not mean that analysts are unanimous in reaching that judgment, or that they are stubbornly arrogant about what they think; it means that they have a lot of good quality information that they and the collectors consider to be reliable. Low confidence means that there isn't much information available, that it is contradictory, and that using different assumptions produces quite different outcomes. One might ask, Why make judgments in which analysts have only low confidence? The answer is, of course, that they have been asked to produce an estimate and that to answer the question requires making judgments even when there is scant information. Moreover, IC analysts are not the only ones who make judgments—or pronouncements—about important issues. Policy makers receive input from many sources in addition to the Intelligence Community, and some of the assessments they receive are stated with much greater confidence or certainty than IC analysts think is warranted. Sometimes it is helpful to address such assertions and to make clear why the IC has less confidence in its accuracy. One of the great failings associated with the Iraq WMD estimate is that those who read it—or, actually, read only the key judgments or, worse, the CIA White Paper that omitted all caveats and alternative judgments—glossed over the clear statement that the judgments were based on very limited information.[28]

Estimates should, and generally do, provide information and judgments on where events are headed, what is driving them, what key actors are trying to accomplish, how they are pursuing their objectives, how long decision makers might have before events cross some threshold (for example, until Iran acquires sufficient fissile material to make a bomb or a fragile government collapses), what to watch for to determine whether events have departed from a particular trajectory, and where/how/when/with whom intervention to change the course of events might be possible. It does other things as well, but these are the key elements. They do not attempt to predict the future, and they should not be construed as an attempt to restrict policy maker options. To the contrary, they are intended to identify opportunities and, sometimes, methods through which the United States might shape events elsewhere in the world.

6 A TALE OF TWO ESTIMATES

THE ERROR-PLAGUED 2002 National Intelligence Estimate (NIE) on Iraq's weapons of mass destruction programs has joined, and for many displaced, failure to predict the fall of the Soviet Union as the quintessential example of Intelligence Community (IC) incompetence.[1] The Iraq estimate was badly flawed, but so was the "system" or "process" through which intelligence was collected, interpreted, and presented to decision makers.[2] Although, as will be argued in the following pages, the estimate per se had no impact on the decision to invade Iraq, it had a profound effect on the scope and shape of efforts to transform the intelligence enterprise made possible by the 9/11 Commission.[3]

Deficient as it was, the Iraq WMD estimate might have remained unread and without impact if rapidly escalating disillusion with the war in Iraq had not triggered the search for scapegoats in Washington's increasingly partisan blame game. The Intelligence Community probably would have explained away the obvious deficiencies of the NIE as the inevitable result of rushing to meet a very short deadline (the ninety-two-page paper was produced in less than three weeks).[4] The fact that the IC could not simply bury the corpse and move on as if it were simply an anomaly was extremely fortunate because much about the intelligence enterprise, especially analytic tradecraft, is much better today than it would have been without the mandate for change catalyzed by the Iraq WMD estimate.[5]

As I argued in the previous chapter, NIEs are diligent and disciplined efforts by the Intelligence Community to assess and interpret fragmentary information on complex issues. Nevertheless, in the run-up to the Iraq war and subsequent political debate they were ascribed near-mythic and talismanic qualities. Individual members of Congress now often proclaim that they need an NIE to make decisions on key issues.[6] Congress has requested more NIEs in the last few years than ever, at least in my thirty-eight years in the IC, and requests from members to produce declassified versions of both key judgments and entire estimates have become much more common.[7] The preparation of estimates is now a subject of heightened interest to journalists, and their existence, not to mention released or leaked findings, is dissected and debated by pundits and media commentators who will never see an NIE.[8]

How long this unusual status will last and whether NIEs will henceforth be read carefully by more than a few administration officials or members of Congress is yet to be determined, but my prediction is "not long" and "not likely." However, during the period that began in the aftermath of the Iraq WMD estimate and continues through the time this is being written, NIEs have been subjected to much closer scrutiny by congressional members and staff, the President's Intelligence Advisory Board (formerly the President's Foreign Intelligence Advisory Board), and senior members of the administration. Given the inflated importance of NIEs and this increased scrutiny, I knew from the beginning of my tenure as deputy director of national intelligence for analysis and chairman of the National Intelligence Council (NIC) that my effectiveness would be judged, in large measure, by the quality and utility of the estimates produced on my watch.[9]

Fortunately, for me at least, the perceived and self-imposed need to improve the quality of NIEs was matched by the mandate and authority delegated to me by Director of National Intelligence John Negroponte.[10] Overstating the matter only slightly, I could mandate changes in the production of NIEs without having to go through the often tortuous bureaucratic procedures required to adopt new guidance and directives governing analytic work elsewhere in the analytic community. This made it possible to implement change quickly, make adjustments as needed, and use NIEs—the flagship product of the analytic community—as a test bed and model for transformational changes affecting all products and agencies.

Most of the estimates produced in the first two years of my tenure were scrutinized closely, and critical readers reported that they were able to see concrete improvement in their quality and utility. We knew, however, that the most significant test of how much we had improved would come when we published our next estimate on Iran's nuclear intentions and capabilities. The reasons for this were many, including that it involved the most lethal weapon of mass destruction in an "Axis of Evil" country and would clearly be seen by many observers as "the next Iraq WMD NIE."[11] In my view, and in the view of many of my senior colleagues, producing an NIE on Iran's nuclear ambitions that could withstand close scrutiny was essential to the success of efforts to restore confidence in our products, our analytic tradecraft, and the Intelligence Community.

In addition to these arguably institutional and professional incentives to "get it right" on Iran, we had both patriotic and personal motivations to do so. Our nation and the Intelligence Community had been embarrassed and tarnished by the way intelligence on Iraq's WMD programs was presented to American decision makers and to the world, and we knew that our findings would be used to inform important U.S. decisions concerning Iran. Personal motivations ranged from the very general—all analysts had been tarred, and morale had been hurt by blowback from the Iraq WMD estimate, and many were eager to redress the situation by doing demonstrably good work—to highly individualistic. I, and three other members of the National Intelligence Board that would determine whether the Iran nuclear estimate was ready, had attended the meeting of the National Foreign Intelligence Board that endorsed the Iraq WMD estimate.[12] I cannot speak for my three colleagues, but I had a personal incentive to avoid making the same mistakes a second time.

The narrative that follows is both an expository and an evolutionary tale of the journey from the 2002 NIE on Iraq's weapons of mass destruction to the 2007 estimate on Iran's nuclear program. As such, it focuses more on context than content to describe how two exceptionally high-profile estimates fit into and were shaped by politics and policy making in Washington during a particular, but not entirely unique, period. In doing so, it will weave together five interactive but analytically discrete strands of developments. One strand examines the genesis and pathology of the Iraq WMD estimate in an attempt to explain why it was written as it was and the lessons learned from postmortems conducted by the Congress, the WMD Commission, and the IC itself. The second strand describes how procedural changes and measures adopted to address systemic problems underscored by the Iraq NIE were incorporated into the production of the Iran nuclear estimate. The exegesis of these estimates constitutes the beginning and end points of the evolutionary process described in a third strand of analysis that attempts to explicate the transition from "bad" to "much better" that occurred between 2002 and late 2007.[13] The fourth and fifth strands involve political tales. One of them focuses on the political context in Washington and how it affected the production of National Intelligence Estimates; the other looks briefly at some of the "people" and ad hominem dimensions of what occurred.

The analysis that follows is a personal and doubtless somewhat idiosyncratic assessment. It is surely incomplete and probably wrong in certain respects, but I have chosen to write it in this way because I made, shaped, or endorsed most of the decisions that constituted and drove the evolutionary process described in the following pages. At one level, this chapter is about what I learned along the way, what I discovered when I looked back at the process to find useful lessons, and what I did to correct the deficiencies I judged to be most injurious to the quality of the product. The transformation of analysis was, of course, a collective undertaking requiring and benefiting from the insights and initiatives of many people. I do not know precisely what lessons my colleagues drew from their participation in the process and will not attempt to speak for them, but my dual positions of deputy director of national intelligence for analysis (DDNI/A) and chairman of the National Intelligence Council meant that the final decisions on most of the issues discussed here were my decisions and, at the risk of sounding egotistical, I think it more useful for readers to understand how I saw and shaped the process than to feign greater objectivity than is warranted. This is, in the end, a personal tale.

GENESIS OF THE IRAQ WMD ESTIMATE

Only President Bush knows when he decided to use military force to overthrow the regime of Saddam Hussein, but by late summer 2002 predictions that he would do so were both widespread and often stated as a near certainty.[14] In mid-August, former National Security Advisor Brent Scowcroft wrote in the *Wall Street Journal* that "leaks of various strategies for an attack on Iraq appear with regularity." His essay was entitled, "Don't Attack Saddam."[15] By early September, members of Congress were urging the president to do a better job of making his case for war against Iraq, and on September 12 President Bush laid out his bill of particulars in his address to the U.N. General Assembly detailing Iraqi duplicity and violation of commitments made to the international community.[16]

The sense that the nation was moving toward war with Iraq was palpable; on September 20, Senator Robert Byrd described the mood as one of "war fervor."[17] It was in this context, and only then, that senators requested a National

Intelligence Estimate on Iraq's weapons of mass destruction. In a series of letters to Director of Central Intelligence George Tenet dated between September 9 and September 17, they asked that the NIE address a number of specific questions about "the current state of Iraq's weapons of mass destruction programs." In negotiations between the Central Intelligence Agency (CIA) and staff of the Senate Select Committee on Intelligence, it was agreed to assign a due date of October 1, 2002.[18]

The ninety-two page estimate was produced very quickly. The first draft was completed on September 23 and discussed, debated, and "coordinated" by agency representatives on September 25. A revised draft was sent to agencies for review on Friday, September 26, and approved by the National Foreign Intelligence Board on October 1. The report was delivered to the Congress on October 3.[19] Although it is tempting to describe what happened as a classic case of "if you want it real bad, you get it real bad," I basically agree with the judgment of the Senate Select Committee on Intelligence that "while more time may have afforded analysts the opportunity to correct some minor inaccuracies in the National Intelligence Estimate (NIE), the Committee does not believe that the fundamental analytical flaws contained in the NIE were the result of the limited time available to the Intelligence Community to complete the Estimate."[20]

The estimate could be produced as quickly as it was because IC analysts, particularly those at the CIA, had been working the issues more or less continuously for some time.[21] Analysis of the issues had been communicated to policy makers in the administration and on the Hill, both orally and in written form, causing Tenet, Deputy National Security Advisor Stephen Hadley, and others to question the need for a National Intelligence Estimate on the subject.[22] Most of the papers and briefings provided to the White House and the Hill were produced by CIA analysts, as was usually the case because of the size of the agency and its assumed and accepted role as the primary source of intelligence support to those senior "customers." I do not know whether the senators who requested an NIE on the subject had concerns about the analysis they had received from the CIA or had learned that other agencies, specifically the State Department's Bureau of Intelligence and Research (INR) and the Department of Energy's Office of Intelligence and Counterintelligence, had different views on Saddam's nuclear weapons program, but they specifically requested "a coordinated, consensus document produced by all relevant components of the Intelligence Community."[23]

A second reason the NIE could be produced quickly was that most of the requested topics had already been treated at length in existing "off the shelf" NIC and CIA products. This was important not only because existing prose could be stitched together and updated as necessary to answer the specific request from the Hill but also, and more importantly, because it was then standard practice in the IC to treat previous NIE judgments, even those on which there had been dissenting views, as of continuing validity unless something had happened or new information had been obtained that made it impossible to simply take what had been "agreed" in the past as the appropriate starting point for new products on the subject. The systemic "problem" was not the ease with which prose from one product could be cut-and-pasted into a new one but the more serious failure routinely and rigorously to review all previous judgments and the underlying intelligence reporting on which they were based.[24] In other words, there was no regularized—or mandatory—procedure to reassess previous judgments in light of new information, including new information about old sources.

In retrospect, I have concluded that two additional factors contributed to the flawed judgments of the Iraq WMD estimate, namely, the context and political environment in which we were working, and the impact of two reports endorsed by DCI Tenet. Although the most exhaustive and influential postmortem analyses of why the Intelligence Community had failed to detect planning and preparations for the attacks on September 11 had not yet been completed, significant "lessons" were already clear and widely discussed by the fall of 2002. One of those lessons was that analysts had been too timid when assessing possibilities and probabilities and insufficiently aggressive when presenting worst-case scenarios.[25] Similar injunctions to be more forward leaning when assessing what "could" happen were implicit in the analysis and recommendations of the Rumsfeld Commission on ballistic missile threats to the United States, and the Jeremiah Report on the Intelligence Community's performance on the Indian nuclear tests of May 1998.[26]

Intelligence Community analysts almost certainly were influenced by specific injunctions to the WMD community (based on the Rumsfeld and Jeremiah reports) to lean forward in their analysis, by the lessons being drawn from examinations of what went "wrong" before 9/11, and by the political atmosphere in Washington characterized by Senator Byrd as "war fervor." This is not to suggest that we were susceptible to "political pressure" or unconsciously pandered to senior policy makers; I believe strongly that was not the case. However, the climate in which we operated at the time, particularly when examining WMD issues, encouraged "worst-case" and "could" (rather than most-likely) judgments. This was probably more subliminal than specific, but it would certainly have been understandable for analysts to err on the side of bad possibilities so they could claim that decision makers had been "warned."

LESSONS LEARNED FROM THE IRAQ WMD ESTIMATE

The Iraq WMD estimate has been thoroughly dissected by the Senate Select Committee on Intelligence and the WMD Commission, so I will not recapitulate their findings here. It will be useful, however, to note some of the key lessons that I learned from those studies and my own rereading of the estimate because those lessons informed my decisions on what to "fix" and how to fix it. I should hasten to add that many others in the Intelligence Community learned essentially the same lessons and that analytic managers in several agencies had already begun to implement corrective measures when I was given the opportunity to lead the effort. This transformed the task from one of persuading people to do something that they thought unnecessary into one of evaluating, harmonizing, and integrating "best practices" to produce a single set of tradecraft guidelines for all agencies. Analysts and senior managers alike were eager to correct deficiencies that had resulted in embarrassing lapses and harsh criticism of our people and our products.

The Iraq WMD estimate was the product of flawed data, flawed analysis, and flawed procedures. As a result, many different, but interrelated, "fixes" were required to reduce the chances of similar errors in the future. The paragraphs that follow will march through what I regard as the most significant lessons with respect to key components of the report and the way it was produced. The lessons are keyed to subtopics of the NIE.

Saddam's Nuclear Weapons Program

In the name of full disclosure, I must make clear that I am not a dispassionate commentator on the nuclear section of the estimate because INR—which, as principal deputy assistant secretary, I represented at the National Foreign Intelligence Board meeting that approved the NIE—strongly dissented from the coordinated judgments of other IC agencies regarding the existence of a reconstituted nuclear weapons program and the interpretation of the evidence used to support those judgments. The INR dissent is noted after the second sentence of the key judgments and elaborated immediately following the key judgments.[27]

The majority judgment that "if left unchecked, it [Iraq] probably will have a nuclear weapon during this decade" rested on seven analytic pillars. Six of those pillars or indicators were spelled out in the key judgments: Saddam's personal interest; Iraq's aggressive attempts to obtain high-strength aluminum tubes, to acquire special magnets, to obtain balancing machines and other specified machine tools, and to reestablish and enhance its cadre of weapons personnel; and activities at several suspect nuclear sites. The seventh, efforts to acquire uranium in Africa, was noted in the text but not in the key judgments. With the exception of "Saddam's personal interest" (all judged that he would like to have nuclear weapons if he could get them), all of the "indicators" had alternative explanations and could plausibly (INR maintained more plausibly) be explained as indicators of something else. The point here is not to crow about who was more correct but, more importantly, to underscore the perils of dismissing alternative hypotheses and alternative judgments.

The problem manifest in the nuclear sections was a more general one, but it was particularly pernicious in those portions of the estimate. That problem, in my view, is that most analysts and agencies approached the topic of nuclear weapons as if they were lawyers building a case rather than as analysts trying to interpret available information. Stated another way, the majority interpreted each of the indicators to support the case that Saddam was reconstituting his nuclear weapons program and disparaged or dismissed alternative interpretations. The key lesson drawn from this point is that individual analysts and the process for producing estimates (and other analytic products) had to develop and examine alternative hypotheses and to articulate clearly why one fit the known information better than the others or to make it clear to readers when the nature of the evidence made it impossible to determine with confidence which alternative was most likely to be true.[28]

The nuclear sections also suffered from the desire of analysts to avoid making the same mistake twice. Inspections of Iraq after the first Gulf War revealed that Saddam had a more varied and more advanced nuclear weapons program than had been suggested by available information or inferred by analysts. In the aftermath of 9/11 and having been criticized for failing to detect Iraq's program before 1991, analysts overvalued Saddam's "denial and deception" capabilities and, in effect, construed the absence of evidence as proving the efficacy of measures to hide what he was assumed to be doing.

Chemical Weapons

The portions of the NIE dealing with chemical weapons were plagued by errors similar to those already described, but I want to focus on three other problems in this section. One involved a variant of the "prove that he is reconstituting his chemical weapons (CW) program" flaw that can be summarized as: "Iraq knows how to manufacture chemical weapons, it produced and used them in the past, and it has the dual-use industrial infrastructure to produce CW should Saddam decide to do so." This logic, in conjunction with Iraq's imputed denial and deception capabilities and record of obstructing inspection of suspect CW facilities, led to a "they must be there even if we cannot find them" approach.[29]

A second flaw involved poor analytic tradecraft on the part of imagery analysts who misread and mischaracterized imagery of a munitions transfer. In short, the principal evidence for what was described as definitive indicator of CW munitions was the presence of a particular type of truck—a water tender—that, in fact, was present when munitions of all kinds were transferred. The erroneous reading of the evidence was compounded by practices that made it unnecessary for specialized analysts to explain how they had reached their conclusions to the analysts who would integrate those judgments into a broader analytic tapestry. The key lesson here is that procedures had to be more transparent and that analysts would "have to show their homework" to their colleagues. "Trust me, I'm a professional" is not the way to do business in the IC; we needed to move to a Reaganesque "trust but verify" approach.

The third problem I want to flag here derives from the fact that analysts are not automatons and do not work in isolation from the political atmosphere of Washington. Like others working in and around the Washington Beltway, analysts were exposed daily to what Senator Byrd characterized as "war fervor." As we were preparing the estimate, I—and I am sure many analysts—were convinced that it was only a matter of time until American troops began the invasion of Iraq. In that atmosphere and with that expectation, there may have been a somewhat stronger disposition to err on the side of warning about the danger that Saddam would employ chemical weapons against our troops than would otherwise have been the case. Objectivity is highly valued in the Intelligence Community, and I doubt that many—or any—consciously skewed their analysis of Saddam's CW capabilities. But analysis is, in the end, a series of judgment calls, and there appears, in retrospect, to have been a bias toward warning of what Saddam *could* have in his CW inventory. This fact of life problem has no easy solution beyond recognizing that analysts are human, that those working in the Intelligence Community are also patriots with a strong sense of camaraderie with those who serve in uniform, and explicitly asking them at key junctures whether they think they might be erring in a particular direction to minimize the risk to our troops.

Biological Weapons

The BW sections of the estimate evinced the problems described in the previous section but had others as well. One that was similar to the "he had and used CW in the past" line of reasoning was enumeration of agents that Iraq *could* be working on and *might* have weaponized. Saddam's implausible explanations for what had happened to some BW reagents and interference with U.N. inspectors were interpreted as supporting the idea that he maintained a secret BW capability. Here, too, his imputed prowess at denial and deception was construed to buttress arguments that he had what we had been unable to discover. It is not always wrong to apply this type of logic, but, when doing so, it must be identified and accompanied by clear distinctions among facts, alleged facts, and assumptions used to close information gaps.[30]

A second, and highly publicized, problem was reliance on reporting from the infamous source known as "Curveball." His reporting claimed that Saddam had developed mobile vans equipped to produce BW agents and that they moved around the country to prevent detection by U.N. inspectors. Collectors learned and have applied many lessons to prevent another Curveball-type incident, but one that directly affects analysts is a requirement first mandated by DCI George Tenet and subsequently broadened by DNI John Negroponte requires that more information about sourcing be revealed to analysts. Initially such information on sourcing was limited to a very few people on the NIC and principal drafters of NIEs, but it has since been extended much more broadly. Knowing how many different sources are reporting on a subject, whether they are being worked by U.S. or foreign collectors, whether the United States has direct access, and similar information is germane to analytic judgments about the reliability of individual reports and the conclusions based on those reports.[31]

The BW sections and subsequent sections on unmanned aerial vehicles (UAVs) evince circular logic that probably would have been caught if more time had been available but might not have been corrected even if it had been. Simply stated, fragmentary evidence and inferences that Saddam had reconstituted a BW program were given greater credibility because, it was claimed, he had developed UAVs to deliver such agents. However, in the section on UAVs, the judgment that they had been developed and were intended for BW dissemination was buttressed by the claim that Iraq had biological weapons. In other words, Saddam must have a BW capability because he had the means to deliver BW, and the purpose of the UAVs must be to deliver BW because he had BW. Each confirmed the existence and purpose of the other, but neither had been confirmed independently.

Unmanned Aerial Vehicles

In addition to the circular logic problem, the section on UAVs was flawed in part because, in the rush to complete the estimate by the agreed deadline and the implicit objective of including virtually everything that seemed to buttress arguments that Saddam still had extensive and expanding WMD programs, materials on software acquisition were introduced at the last minute even though few analysts or agencies had a chance to look at, let alone think about, the information. We now know that the information and the way it was construed were completely wrong, but the drive to include "everything and the kitchen sink" meant that they were made part of the bill of particulars against Iraq. The lesson from this is clear: If new information becomes available, it should not be introduced into an estimate (or other product) before it has been properly assessed. Moreover, if the information deals with something that is important, production of the estimate should be delayed until we understand what we have and what it means. Leaping ahead in the story, this is precisely what we did in the case of the 2007 Iran nuclear NIE; we stopped the process during review of the penultimate draft because we obtained new information with the clear potential to change important judgments.

PROCESS FLAWS

In addition to the specific deficiencies cited in the previous section—and others detailed in the SSCI and WMD Commission reports—the Iraq WMD estimate reflected and underscored a number of shortcomings in the way estimates and many other products were produced. These process flaws arguably were more important than were the factual and analytical errors in the estimate because they were indicative of broader problems in the way IC agencies prepared and presented analytical products. Some have been mentioned previously but warrant additional discussion.

As previously noted, the Iraq WMD estimate was constructed by stitching together and updating arguments and judgments from previously coordinated products and materials produced by a single agency, in most cases the CIA. The use of "off-the-shelf" products was expedient—it would have been impossible to conduct a zero-based analysis of the intelligence on Iraq's WMD programs in the short time allotted—but it was also a "logical" way to proceed given DCI Tenet's initial position that it was unnecessary to produce an NIE on the subject because it had been adequately covered in other documents.[32] Proceeding in this way had the advantage of "consistency" and speed but effectively precluded careful reexamination of the validity of the intelligence used to support previously reached judgments to determine whether new information confirmed or conflicted with what was known previously and whether subsequent information had raised or reduced concerns about the knowledge or veracity of specific sources. It also effectively stacked the deck against dissenting and alternative views.

I want to be very clear about the point made in the previous sentence—that is, that it was the process followed, not personalities or "politicization," that stacked the deck in favor of previously articulated judgments and agreed positions and against arguments that challenged those judgments. This particular problem probably could not have been avoided in the case of the Iraq WMD estimate, given the short deadline, but it could have been mitigated more effectively (see the following discussion). The way in which the process was biased in favor of status quo ante judgments may be summarized by noting that they were carried forward unless a convincing case had been made that they were no longer appropriate. Making the case for change is more difficult if only some of those working the problem have reexamined old evidence and judgments. Understandable reluctance to change a judgment, thereby admitting error, was reinforced by a process that made some analysts and agencies de facto defenders of the status quo and put an unreasonable burden on those who had done the additional hard work to persuade persons who had not been a part of that effort that they should accept conclusions reached without their participation. The problem was further compounded by rivalries and mythology ascribing greater or lesser wisdom to particular agencies. The critical determinant must be the quality of the argument, not who makes it.

The broader lesson that I want to highlight is that off-the-shelf products and previous judgments must not be treated as if they embodied divine writ and sacred text. They are simply the best judgments of analysts working with the information available to them at a particular point in time. If the issue is important—and almost by definition, any issue that warrants treatment as a National Intelligence Estimate is important—the better way to proceed is to go back to square one with an open mind and determination to reexamine all judgments, underlying assessments, and supporting evidence. As a practical matter, most of the sources and judgments are likely to be reaffirmed, but that should be the result of rigorous tradecraft, not assumed ab initio. To implement this lesson, I mandated zero-based reviews for all estimates.

The need to reexamine old information in light of subsequent intelligence subsumes a second lesson from the Iraq WMD estimate, namely, the need to accord analysts greater insight into the nature of the intelligence provided by collectors. As already noted, this was one of the first lessons identified and codified in the form of new procedures. Heretofore the wall between analysts and collectors (or operators) had been quite high and relatively impermeable. Overstating the situation only slightly, analysts could ask for more information but could not ask many questions about the sources or methods that had provided the intelligence made available to them and had no choice but to accept at face value the judgment of collectors regarding the access and veracity of their sources. Parenthetically, this is one of the reasons most analysts like diplomatic reporting—one always knows where it came from and that the person conveying the information wanted it to be made available to the U.S. government. That did not necessarily ensure that it was accurate, but it did reflect what the individual or organization involved wanted U.S. officials to hear.

Shortly after the flaws of the Iraq WMD estimate became apparent, Tenet mandated that the preparation of estimates henceforth include a formal written statement from the head of each collection component attesting that all of the intelligence from that component that had been used in the estimate had been reevaluated and that the results of that reevaluation were made known to those preparing the estimate. This formal statement is still required, but over time the process has evolved in a way that make collectors more integral participants in the production of the estimates themselves, alerting analysts when specific reports have been or are being reevaluated, especially when they are now judged to be less reliable than previously indicated, and answering questions about the number of different sources in a particular reporting stream, for example. The resultant changes to the process have had a number of beneficial consequences, not least of which are greater standardization of criteria and terminology for assigning judgments of reliability and greater clarity and consistency in the assignment of confidence levels to specific key judgments.[33] As is the case in most areas of reform, progress has been significant but insufficient.

A third process flaw, albeit one that was unique rather than generic, was the simultaneous release of an unclassified White Paper on the subject that differed, in important respects, from the Iraq WMD estimate. The bottom line lesson from this chapter of the Iraq WMD saga is that any declassified versions of a National Intelligence Estimate must accurately and as completely as possible reflect what is said in the classified text. That lesson was ultimately codified in the form of guidance from Director of National Intelligence Mike McConnell that played a key role in the brouhaha surrounding the release of declassified key judgments from the Iran nuclear estimate, but that part of the story will be deferred until later in the tale. Here I want to focus on what happens when Intelligence Community judgments become part of the public debate on complex, contentious, and partisan issues.

In his letter to DCI Tenet requesting the production of "a coordinated, consensus document produced by all relevant components of the Intelligence Community," Senator Richard Durbin also asked the DCI to "produce an unclassified summary of this NIE . . . so the American public can better understand this important issue."[34] In subsequent years, requests for unclassified summaries or entire NIEs became almost commonplace, but I certainly do not recall that being the case or being asked to consider producing an unclassified version of any of the hundred or more estimates that I reviewed during my years in the INR front office, most of them as deputy assistant secretary for analysis. Nor do I recall a discussion of whether or how to declassify the Iraq WMD estimate when the National Foreign Intelligence Board considered it. The estimate per se was not declassified at the time, but Senator Durbin's request was honored with the delivery of a White Paper entitled "Iraq's Weapons of Mass Destruction Programs."[35]

The genesis of the White Paper and the ways in which it differed from—and conveyed a different impression than—the Iraq WMD estimate are described at length in Section X of the SSCI Report on the Intelligence Community's prewar assessments on Iraq.[36] Here I want to focus on context, consequences, and broader lessons. One part of that context was the prospect—in September 2002 many would have said the likelihood—that the president would order the use of military force against a nation that had not attacked the United States or one of our allies. "Intelligence" and "intelligence judgments" provided the public rationale for taking preemptive action, creating a perceived need to "share" at least some of the intelligence with the American public. Simply stated, the White House wanted to release certain intelligence-derived information to make its case for war, and members of Congress wanted to do so to explain why they would give or withhold approval for what the president wanted to do.

What became the White Paper on Iraq's WMD programs was initiated by a request to the Deputy Director of Central Intelligence from the National Security Council Deputies Committee.[37] The task was assigned to the National Intelligence Council in May 2002. Like the estimate, the draft drew heavily on existing papers and reflected what was being shared with administration officials and the Congress. Production of the White Paper languished through the spring and summer, in part because no deadline had been assigned, but also, I believe, because the nature of the request made clear that the goal was to make a strong case that Saddam's WMD posed a serious and urgent threat to American interests. As an art form, White Papers generally are policy documents prepared by the executive branch to explain and justify what it wants to do. At least some in the Intelligence Community were uncomfortable with the assignment. Moreover, it was difficult to make a very compelling case at the unclassified level, especially when including information on information gaps, contradictory intelligence, and other caveats appropriate to an IC assessment.

Whatever the original intent of those who commissioned the White Paper, what actually happened was that it was rushed to completion after approval of the Iraq WMD estimate to satisfy requests for an unclassified paper on the subject. It was *not* a coordinated product, and it was *not* a declassified version of the NIE, but it was widely characterized or interpreted as being precisely that. In addition to sharing most of the analytic flaws of the NIE, the White Paper had two egregious shortcomings of its own. One was the omission of caveats and qualifiers similar to those included in the NIE to distinguish "fact" from "judgment" and to indicate how confident analysts were of the judgments they had reached. As a result, it came across as far more definitive than was the estimate. The second consequential flaw was that it did not make clear the nature or implications of the dissenting and alternative views highlighted in the estimate. Indeed, the wording of the White Paper obscured the significance of the analytic disagreements.

The omission of qualifiers and obscuring of analytic differences are serious flaws because they convey to the reader a higher level of knowledge and confidence in the judgments than is warranted. Estimates are precisely that; best-effort attempts to interpret, explain, and anticipate on the basis of imperfect knowledge of capabilities, intentions, and many other critical variables.

Any product that fails to make clear the limitations of what is known or the existence of credible alternative ways to interpret what is known conveys an unwarranted degree of certainty. Policy makers and all others supported by the Intelligence Community need to know the caveats and limitations of analytical products. Often, understanding why analytic differences exist is more important than who has articulated a particular view or what interpretation ultimately proves to be most correct. If the ice under a judgment is thin, decision makers need to know that; and if good analysts using the same information reach different conclusions, it should be self-evident that one cannot have high confidence in either or any of the alternative judgments. The intelligence reform legislation mandate to conduct alternative analysis and *Intelligence Community Directive 203: Analytic Standards* aim to ensure that this deficiency is corrected.

The unclassified White Paper may have had another deleterious consequence as well. Its existence and the facts that it was shorter than the NIE and was widely construed as the unclassified version of the estimate may have caused members of Congress to conclude that it was unnecessary for them to read the highly classified (and therefore much more inconvenient to read and use) analysis of the subject. Whether it was greater convenience (to read highly classified papers, members—not staff, most of whom do not have the requisite clearances—must go to one of the few secure facilities to read and must remember what they can and cannot say publicly) or because they believed that the White Paper accurately and adequately reflected the judgments—and confidence levels—of the longer estimate, few members appear to have read the NIE before voting to authorize the use of military force against Iraq. Writing in *The Washington Post*, Dana Priest reported in 2004 that no more than six senators had read the classified estimate.[38] *The Hill* magazine reported a higher figure (twenty-two) based on a survey of senators conducted in 2007.[39] Although it is impossible to say whether the vote to authorize the use of military force against Iraq would have been different if more members had read the NIE, it is at least interesting to note that nine of the twenty-two members who claimed to have done so voted against the resolution (compared to only fourteen of the seventy-seven who did not claim to have read the NIE).[40]

Available information does not tell us why those who read the NIE voted as they did, but the estimate's qualifiers, caveats, and explication of dissenting views may have influenced some of them. Despite its many and serious flaws, the Iraq WMD estimate raised a number of caution flags that should have been obvious even to readers who did not get beyond the key judgments. They include:

- We *judge* that Iraq has continued its weapons of mass destruction (WMD) programs.
- We *lack specific information* on many key aspects of Iraq's WMD programs.
- We *assess* that Saddam does not yet have nuclear weapons or sufficient material to make any.
- We *assess* that Baghdad has begun renewed production of mustard, sarin . . .
- Although *we have little specific information* on Iraq's CW stockpile . . .
- We *judge* Iraq has some lethal and incapacitating BW agents . . .
- We have *low confidence in our ability to assess* when Saddam would use WMD.
- Baghdad for now *appears* to be drawing a line short of conducting terrorist attacks with conventional or CBW against the United States . . .
- INR's *alternative view* of Iraq's nuclear program . . .
- The Air Force *view* that Iraq was developing UAVs primarily for reconnaissance, not for delivery of CBW agents . . .[41] (Emphasis added.)

The reason for enumerating some of the qualifiers and noting the fact that a much higher percentage of senators who read the NIE voted against the use of force resolution than was the case for those who did not claim to have read it is not to make the case that the estimate was less bad than is conventionally believed to be the case but to underscore the need for better communication between the Intelligence Community and those it supports to ensure that messages are received as they are intended and that decision makers need to understand the qualifications and limitations of estimative analysis. In the case of the Iraq WMD estimate, the most accurate summary statement should have been, "We judge that Iraq is reconstituting its WMD capabilities but do not know that it has done so and do not know with certainty or specificity how much has been reconstituted or how long it will take to complete the process."

It is not the purpose of this paper to examine when or why the president made the decision to invade Iraq or why members of Congress voted as they did when asked to authorize the use of military force. I am confident, however, that the flawed NIE per se did not play a significant role in those decisions. Despite political posturing both before and after the estimate was written,

I am aware of no evidence that the NIE persuaded the administration to invade Iraq when it did. As previously noted, administration officials had already received, considered, and commented on intelligence judgments on Iraq WMD, most of them provided by the CIA months before publication of the NIE. Members of Congress had been briefed, again, mostly by the CIA, on the same analytic conclusions about Saddam's WMD.

How much of that information registered, how many read the analytic products that were regularly sent to the Hill by the CIA and other components of the Intelligence Community, and how many were swayed by the definitive character of the unclassified White Paper that, like the classified estimate, was delivered to the Congress a week before the vote to authorize the use of force is unknown, at least to me. But Washington is quintessentially a political town that needed a scapegoat to blame when the war went badly, no weapons of mass destruction were found, public opinion began to turn against the war, and political debate became even more partisan. The NIE's obvious flaws made it a perfect candidate and, not surprisingly, far more effort has been devoted to describing and decrying the estimate's defects and IC incompetence than to examining why officials made the decisions that they did.

Political outrage, both real and feigned, generally has a very short half-life in Washington. This time was different. Even though the Iraq WMD estimate had little influence on the decision to go to war, there is no question that it was wrong on a number of issues critical to our nation's foreign and security policies. Just how wrong was confirmed by the interim (October 2003) and final (September 2004) reports of the Iraq Survey Group, the report issued by the Senate Select Committee on Intelligence (July 2004), and the report of the Commission on the Intelligence Capabilities of the United States Regarding Weapons of Mass Destruction (also known as the WMD Commission and the Silberman-Robb Commission, March 2005).[42] The high profile and clear deficiencies of IC work on Iraq WMD, specific recommendations to address those deficiencies, and the political momentum generated and sustained by the 9/11 Commission converged to produce the Intelligence Reform and Terrorism Prevention Act of 2004. Changes mandated by that legislation and, as importantly, the determination of senior analytic managers in the Intelligence Community to correct the obvious deficiencies made it both necessary and possible to make fundamental changes in the way the IC prepares and presents analytical findings.

APPLYING LESSONS, IMPROVING THE PROCESS, AND IMPROVING THE PRODUCT

Even though the quality of analytic tradecraft in the Iraq WMD estimate was inferior to most of the work produced by the National Intelligence Council and the IC more generally, it was not a complete anomaly. The NIE may have been—and I believe was—uniquely bad, but most of its flaws were present, to some extent, in many analytic products.[43] Our task, therefore, was to "fix" the entire analytic enterprise. I decided to approach this task as a challenge with both top-down and bottom-up dimensions. Full explication of what we did, why we followed the selected approach, how we accomplished what we did, and what remains to be achieved would greatly expand the length of this chapter and digress too far from its focus on two watershed estimates, but it will be useful to summarize some of the lessons and corrective measures that were particularly germane to the focus of this chapter.

The first lesson learned and applied was the importance of systematic re-evaluation and, as appropriate, recharacterization of intelligence information (so-called raw intelligence) prepared and provided by collectors. Such reevaluations were conducted on a routine basis, but the results were not routinely shared with the analytical community, and there was no regular linkage between the reviews and the production of a National Intelligence Estimate. George Tenet took important steps to address this deficiency shortly after it became apparent how wrong the Iraq WMD estimate was and how badly U.S. leadership and the stature of the Intelligence Community had been damaged by the flawed intelligence used by Secretary of State Colin Powell when presenting the U.S. case to the U.N. Security Council.[44] Those steps included mandating that the heads of collection agencies formally vouch for all information used in NIEs that had been provided by their agencies and that analysts preparing estimates receive more information on the provenance of the information.

I do not know whether any of the collectors objected to these new procedures, but they had become part of the normal NIE process before I became chairman of the National Intelligence Council in May 2005. The procedures continued to evolve in the years between my arrival at the NIC and publication of the Iran nuclear NIE in December 2007. That evolution resulted in much closer (albeit still insufficient) collaboration between analysts and collectors at all stages of the production process and in the routinization of procedures to ensure that old information was reevaluated through comparison with newer information and that new information was assessed in terms of how well it tracked with what had been learned previously. The goal was not simply to determine which was true or false but to cross-check information and highlight alternative possibilities. As will be described in the following pages, by the time we produced the Iran nuclear estimate, the requirement to conduct zero-based reevaluations of all sources, the information provided by those sources, and the judgments based on what those sources said had become a major undertaking.

A second lesson was that other means of conveying intelligence information and analytic judgments to policy makers are more important than are National Intelligence Estimates. By the time most estimates are produced, decision makers working on the issue have already received a great deal of information on the subject, including both raw intelligence and analytic products but also including briefings from and conversations with the analysts with whom they interact on a regular basis. The oft-repeated assertion that policy makers do not read NIEs is both true and easily understandable. Those who are working the issue should—and usually do—know basically what it is going to say, and those who are not working on the issue are too busy to bother with things outside their purview.[45] This does not make NIEs unimportant (why they are important is discussed in Chapter 5), but it does mean that simply "fixing the NIE problem" would not adequately address the need to improve the quality of intelligence input to the decision-making process.

Improving the quality of the IC analytic enterprise requires several interconnected streams of development, no one of which can be fully successful unless there is progress on all dimensions. Oversimplifying for the sake of brevity, I decided that the best way to improve the performance of the IC as a whole was to improve the performance of individual analysts and each of the analytic components of the Community. Essential requisites for doing so were to improve training, tradecraft, and transparency.

Training involves multiple dimensions and is essential for many reasons. One dimension requires developing or deepening expertise on the growing number of highly complex issues on which policy makers expect support from the Intelligence Community.[46] This is partially a matter of career development— assigning analysts to accounts that use their expertise and experience, leaving them on accounts long enough to deepen their knowledge of the subject, and developing career paths that build on what they already know while broadening or further deepening their expertise. Doing so is necessary because most agencies adapted to the uncertainties of the early post–Cold War era by optimizing flexibility by requiring analysts to move frequently from one account to another, thereby emphasizing variety at the expense of building specialized knowledge. In other words, we were training utility infielders rather than late inning relief pitchers.

A second dimension of the training challenge derives from the demographics of the Intelligence Community in general and the analytic community in particular. As a result of downsizing, rightsizing, hiring freezes, and the like in the 1990s, the age profile of the community is skewed toward the upper and lower ends of the spectrum with relatively few baby boomers at the high end, roughly 60 percent having joined the IC after 9/11, and very few in the middle. The IC's traditional guildlike approach to training and mentoring is completely inadequate to meet the need to move most of the workforce rapidly up the learning curve. We need new ways to inculcate tradecraft skills, substantive knowledge, and managerial competencies.

Another dimension of the training challenge is to ensure that analysts understand and know how to apply analytic techniques. For most, this involves reinforcing elements of the disciplinary training they received in college and graduate school, but it also must ensure that all analysts understand what is necessary to prevent the kinds of analytic flaws highlighted by postmortems of the Iraq WMD estimate. The rationale is both simple and straightforward; if we are going to hold individuals (and agencies) accountable for the quality of their analytic tradecraft, we must ensure that they have been given the requisite skills and know how to apply them. Initial steps toward this objective include a new course called "Analysis 101" (now called "Critical Thinking and Structured Analysis") that was developed by my Analytic Integrity and Standards team in conjunction with training specialists from across the IC and follow on instruction in each agency.[47] One of the minimum goals of this training is to ensure that analysts from all agencies have received the same high-quality instruction. Much of the training, like Analysis 101, is given in classes with students from across the Community. This "joint training" allows them to network and facilitates collaboration and divisions of labor because analysts and managers can now be confident that colleagues elsewhere have been trained to the same levels and are evaluated using the same criteria.[48]

Analytic tradecraft is the shorthand reference to a bundle of practices codified in *Intelligence Community Directive 203: Analytic Standards* and *Intelligence Community Directive 206: Sourcing Requirements for Disseminated*

Analytic Products.[49] The standards were developed to meet requirements mandated by the December 2004 intelligence reform legislation to correct deficiencies revealed by the Iraq WMD estimate. They include:

- Properly describe quality and reliability of sources.
- Properly caveat and express uncertainties or confidence in analytic judgments.
- Properly distinguish between underlying intelligence and analyst's assumptions and judgments.
- Incorporate alternative analysis where appropriate.
- Employ logical argumentation.
- Demonstrate consistency with previous judgments or highlight changes.

In addition to their centrality in training programs, these and related standards also constitute the criteria used to evaluate the quality of analytic products. Individual agencies use the standards to evaluate their own performance and/or to determine when products are ready for publication. They also are used to evaluate assessments produced by all analytic components on selected topics; the results of these evaluations are reported to the Congress each year.[50]

A central feature of the tradecraft standards is the need for transparency—readers must be able to follow and, if appropriate, reconstruct the logic of the argument, the assumptions used to close information gaps, the assessed reliability and "weights" assigned to different sources, and why particular sources and alternative hypotheses were judged to be less persuasive. Stated differently, analysts must "show their homework," and their analyses must be "reproducible" in the sense that a scientific experiment can be replicated to determine whether others achieve the same results.

Possibly the most important dimensions of transparency—and this judgment is one of the lessons I draw from the case of the Iraq WMD estimate (to include the many elements previously noted)—is the need for clear explication of what is known, what is deduced or inferred, what is assumed, and anything else that is critical to the argument of the analysis. A related dimension is the need to make clear to recipients of the intelligence when, how, and why analysts with access to the same information reach different judgments. If weighing the information differently or using different assumptions to close gaps leads logically to different conclusions, that fact must be revealed to policy makers as soon as it is known. The need to do so was one of the first lessons that I implemented as deputy director of national intelligence for analysis and chairman of the NIC.

Drawing and implementing lessons learned from postmortems on the Iraq WMD case was important, but it was not and should not have been the primary goal. The primary goal, in my view, was a compound one containing a number of interconnected elements. Improving the quality of intelligence support to the national security enterprise was obviously of great importance. If we did not improve the quality and utility of the intelligence we collected and the interpretations of that intelligence we provided to those we support did not improve, none of the other changes made in response to requirements specified in the intelligence reform legislation or initiated by me and other leaders of the Intelligence Community would have been worth the effort.

The adoption and implementation of tradecraft standards made it possible to track, and to some extent measure, improvements in the product, but quality improvement per se would have been insufficient. We not only had to make the product better, we had to be seen to have made it better. Stated somewhat differently, we had to regain the confidence of those we support—in the executive branch, the Congress, and in allied and partner governments. Paraphrasing an old advertising slogan, we had to earn the confidence of officials who believed that they had been burned by the Intelligence Community and, in some cases, had invested much political capital in the public criticism of IC analytic products. The task of regaining confidence was compounded by incessant cheap shots from media commentators who in most cases had never seen an IC product but had no incentive to abandon laugh lines that still get a response.[51]

Recognizing that this was the case, I made it my highest priority to restore confidence in IC analysts and our work by demonstrating clear and consistent improvement—to the White House and others in the executive branch, the Congress, the President's Intelligence Advisory Board (PIAB), and ourselves. I resolved to do this, in part, by moving quickly to formulate and implement new tradecraft standards and other measures to correct the substantive and procedural deficiencies highlighted by the Iraq WMD case and by ensuring that members and staff of our oversight committees and the PIAB knew what we were doing and that we had a plan, were moving out smartly to implement that plan, and intended to refine the plan as we went along rather than attempt to get it completely right the first time. We helped those we had to convince by telling them what to look for in our products and by pointing out how we were doing things differently when invited to provide oral briefings. For the most part, critics and skeptics became attentive monitors who wanted us to succeed and gradually began to provide positive feedback that helped enormously with the morale problems exacerbated by the way all analysts were tarred with the Iraq WMD brush.

Even with a strong mandate to transform many aspects of the way the Intelligence Community conducts business, the wheels of progress often turned very slowly. This was true with respect to many elements of reform, even those that enjoyed widespread support. My basic approach to analytic transformation was to consult, identify best practices, pilot ideas, foster champions, and obtain buy in before making them mandatory. The downside to this approach is that it takes time, and time was something that I did not have in abundance. Perhaps the easiest way to underscore this point is to cite the conversation that I had with then Chair of the House Permanent Select Committee on Intelligence Peter Hoekstra roughly ten days after I had assumed my new positions in the Office of the Director of National Intelligence. After I outlined my vision and approach, both of which were pretty rudimentary at that point, he asked what he could do to help. When I responded that I needed time to effect transformational changes without breaking anything, he interrupted me to say that time was one thing that he could not give me. As far as he was concerned, I had to move quickly and demonstrate that I was doing so. I heard him, and though it was more than a bit annoying to be told less than two weeks into the job that I needed to move more quickly, I understood immediately that I would be operating in a political context that put a premium on speed. Stated another way, Congress thought it had "fixed" problems in the Intelligence enterprise by passing reform legislation, and failure to demonstrate concrete results almost immediately would be interpreted as incompetence or bureaucratic intransigence. I was reminded of the statement in the report of the WMD Commission noting the Intelligence Community's almost perfect record of resisting external recommendations.[52]

On reflection, I realized that there was a fortuitous convergence between the authorities I had by virtue of my two formal positions and the opportunity to change analytic tradecraft across the Intelligence Community by mandating changes to its two flagship products: National Intelligence Estimates and the President's Daily Brief (PDB). DNI John Negroponte had delegated responsibility for both to me; to initiate changes in either, I needed only his concurrence. I proposed to direct that both the PDB and NIEs immediately begin to incorporate specified changes, such as the exploration of alternative hypotheses and clear explication of analytic differences. Negroponte approved my proposal, and the changes went into affect right away.

Resistance to making the directed changes was minimal, in part because other senior analytic managers recognized the need to improve the tradecraft employed in these products. Making the changes to the PDB was important for many reasons, not least of which is that doing so, in conjunction with its transformation from an exclusively CIA product to a Community product (albeit one in which CIA's preponderance of all-source analysts continued to draft the most contributions), addressed what I regarded as one of the most important process problems identified by the Iraq WMD postmortems. Given how hard it is to change the thinking of senior officials after they have already received, internalized, and spoken or acted on the basis of information conveyed via a mechanism such as the PDB, getting it right the first time, and making clear the limitations of what we know and the existence of alternative interpretations, is essential. We now do this better than we did.

Making these and other changes to the PDB and NIEs had additional and equally important impacts on analytical production across the IC. The fact that they were regarded as the most prestigious, if not always the most important, Community publications made it easy to use them as positive role models. If using specified methods of analytic tradecraft was appropriate for these products, why would analysts and agencies want to employ different standards for other assessments? In other words, mandating changes to these flagship products redefined the standard against which other products were measured, and it did so more quickly, and probably more effectively, than formal adoption—almost two years later—of an Intelligence Community directive mandating new procedures.[53]

Two downstream benefits flowing from the mandated changes to the PDB and NIEs warrant special mention. By virtue of the fact that the preparation of NIEs necessarily involves participation by analysts from all agencies with expertise on the subject being addressed (which, as a practical matter, usually means that all but a few agencies participate), it provided an excellent platform for demonstrating and teaching how to apply the new analytic standards. Over time, dozens of analysts from across the IC participated in these substantive tutorials and were able to share with their home agency colleagues how to apply them and why it was important to do so. The second benefit was that analytic managers gradually realized that it was more convenient to employ one set of standards—that required for publication in the PDB and for submission of drafts to the National Intelligence Council—than to have one set for the premier publications and another for their own products. As a result, multiple independent decisions to simplify the review process and mentoring their junior analysts by making "my" standards "their" standards effected change more quickly and with less disgruntlement than could have been achieved in other ways.

Ability to act quickly, opportunity to address critical deficiencies highlighted by the postmortems, and desire to capitalize on the demonstration effects of doing things differently with respect to the PDB and NIEs were important reasons for focusing first on those two product lines, but they were not my most important motivation for doing so. The most important incentive was my sense of the political environment and conviction that we had to show results if we were to regain the trust and confidence of those we support and those with oversight responsibilities. In this respect, I was playing to three primary audiences: senior members of the administration, congressional oversight committees and the President's Intelligence Advisory Board (PIAB), and senior officials of the Intelligence Community.

The primary vehicle for reaching senior administration officials is the PDB. Although these officials acceded to rather than led the drive for intelligence reform, there was no doubt in my mind that we had blotted our copybook with our most important customers. We had to regain their confidence, and the most important way to do so was to improve the PDB.[54] For reasons having more to do with the intense focus on the Iraq WMD estimate than with their historic importance, congressional oversight committees and PIAB members had made NIEs the most important indicator of IC analytic competence. Regardless of how often or how closely they read NIEs, or how much improvement was made in other analytic products, estimates were going to be, for some time at least, the litmus test for assessing IC performance. If we did not demonstrate steady and significant improvement in the tradecraft of NIEs, we—I—would have been judged to have failed. If we were judged to be making progress with respect to NIEs, we would buy time and latitude to effect changes in other areas.

Senior officials of the Intelligence Community comprised the third primary audience. As members of the National Intelligence Board, which determined when estimates were ready for dissemination, they have a personal as well as an institutional stake in the quality of and verdict on NIEs. An estimate judged by policy makers and/or overseers to be seriously flawed besmirched their reputations as well as my own and that of the NIC. Moreover, as already noted, four members of the NIB during the period covered by this paper had also been on the National Foreign Intelligence Board that approved the much-criticized Iraq estimate. Getting it right was, for some, a personal as well as a professional goal. But this group constituted a target audience for other reasons as well. All were friends and long-time colleagues, but not all were enthusiastic about some of the other changes I was trying to make in my capacity as deputy director of national intelligence for analysis.[55] Building credibility and confidence through positive reception of NIEs probably helped me; poor reactions to NIEs certainly would have made it harder to accomplish other objectives for which I needed their cooperation and support.

What was true in a general sense for all NIEs was true in spades for the one on Iran's nuclear intentions and capabilities that we began in 2006. For many reasons—because it dealt with one type of WMD and therefore would provide a ready basis for comparison to the Iraq WMD estimate; because it was undertaken in an increasingly and bitterly partisan political context; because many, especially in the Congress, expected that the judgments of the NIE would be critical inputs into policy decisions on Iran; and because it was an obvious candidate for assessing whether the IC had learned and applied lessons from the Iraq WMD postmortem—we expected this estimate to be scrutinized very closely. If this estimate was judged to have been incompetently prepared, there was a real danger that everything else we had accomplished and the many fragile but promising reforms just beginning to gain traction would be disparaged or ignored. We had to get this one right, and we had to be seen to have gotten it right. The stakes were that high.

IRAN'S NUCLEAR INTENTIONS AND CAPABILITIES

There are essentially three reasons for undertaking production of a National Intelligence Estimate: A policy maker asks for it, new information makes it appropriate or imperative to revisit and update issues examined previously, or IC seniors—typically but not always those serving on the National Intelligence Council—become uncomfortable repeating judgments on important issues that have not been reexamined for more than a few years or, in some cases, months. Willingness to prepare an NIE is also a function of competing demands for the time of national intelligence officers and others with the requisite expertise. Although the Intelligence Community is large, the number of analysts with expertise appropriate for most NIE topics is quite small, and, for reasons suggested in the preceding section, the bar for participation on the prospective Iran nuclear estimate was raised higher than normal.[56]

When I agreed to launch a new estimate on Iran's nuclear activities in late 2006, I did so because Iran was pressing ahead with its centrifuge program despite international efforts to dissuade it from doing so. The combination of Iranian progress and intransigence naturally led to questions of the "How long before Iran gets the bomb?" variety that made it appropriate for us to reassess our time lines. A second reason was that some of my senior analysts were uneasy about justifying current judgments on the basis of information that was, in some cases, several years old. It was time to take another look at the issues and the intelligence that formed the basis for our judgments. My third reason was that I was confident that we were ready for the "prime time" scrutiny the estimate was certain to receive. Changes that we had implemented over the preceding eighteen months were taking hold, and I had been quite pleased by the tradecraft and quality of other products prepared under the auspices of the NIOs for weapons of mass destruction and for the Middle East. At this time, my reasons for doing so did not yet include requests and pressure from the Congress stimulated by concern that the administration was preparing to invade Iran.[57] That came later. One of the first manifestations of this concern was the inclusion of a requirement for "a comprehensive National Intelligence Estimate on Iran" to be submitted not later than ninety days after the date of enactment of the FY2007 Defense Authorization Act.[58] To make the task more manageable, we ultimately reached agreement to produce three specialized estimates rather than a single comprehensive one.

This was a very big undertaking because of the volume of material available. The Intelligence Community had stepped up efforts to collect intelligence on Iran, and those efforts were beginning to yield results. The effort involved the reevaluation of all previous judgments and the intelligence reports on which they were based. The initial draft of the estimate on nuclear activities was approximately 150 pages long, but its judgments were essentially the same as those presented in the May 2005 "Memorandum to Holders" on Iran's nuclear program. "Memorandum to Holders" is a term of art used to indicate an "update" to a previous NIE that considers information obtained subsequent to publication of the latest estimate on a subject without a zero-based review of all previous judgments and intelligence.

Over the next several weeks, the draft was subjected to rigorous peer review within the NIC and reorganized, revised, and clarified before beginning the formal process known as "coordination." Each of the agencies participating in the coordination process reviewed the draft independently, and representatives of these agencies attended multiday sessions to discuss and debate all aspects of the document. The draft was revised and again submitted for formal coordination. It went through this cycle several times. The "penultimate" draft delivered to me in early June essentially reconfirmed, albeit with somewhat greater clarity, the judgments of the 2005 update. We were preparing to schedule a meeting of the National Intelligence Board to consider the estimate when the availability of new information caused us to halt the process until we determined what we had and whether it would be necessary to revise any of our judgments.

The years-long effort to acquire additional intelligence began to produce significant new streams of information in the first half of 2007. At first, we did not know exactly what we had because the new information had not yet been evaluated and cross-checked to determine whether it was reliable. Those who had demanded and were expecting a new estimate on Iran's nuclear capabilities were not happy when told that we would have to delay completion until we had evaluated and, as appropriate, incorporated the new information.

Over the next several weeks, NIO for Weapons of Mass Destruction Vann Van Diepen and I met with several members of Congress, some of them numerous times. We did so sometimes together, sometimes individually, and sometimes accompanied by analysts with expertise on a particular set of issues. In these sessions, we provided the same updates on what we were learning about and from the new intelligence that were being provided to senior administration officials. In my view, these briefings were well received. That they were—or the extent to which they were—attests, I believe, to the success of our efforts to restore confidence in our competence and integrity. It was reassuring to hear, as I did on a number of occasions, some variant of the phrase, "OK. I trust you." I know that this was, in part, a statement about me but choose to believe that it was also an inclusive use of the word "you," referring to the NIC and at least some other elements of the Intelligence Community. We had begun to dig ourselves out of the very deep hole created by the Iraq WMD estimate.

The new intelligence streams were extremely fragile, and it is appalling that someone or some individuals felt compelled to speculate or brag about them.

I will not comment except to say that I find it extremely distressing that any member of the Intelligence or Policy Community would violate the law, personal pledges (oaths) to protect such information, and professional ethics in such a manner. In my view, doing this one time warrants loss of clearances and immediate dismissal.

Working our way through the new information required another zero-based scrub of all reporting and all of the judgments potentially affected by the newly acquired intelligence. We used details in old reporting to assess the new information and used the new information to check the accuracy and reliability of previous holdings. Among the many questions we had to address was whether the newly acquired information was genuine or had been fed to us to mislead us. Consistent with the new procedures, we conducted multiple and independent checks and ultimately included several "alternative hypotheses" regarding the new information and what it told us about Iran's intentions and capabilities in an annex to the main text of the NIE. We checked and double-checked the information every way that we could think to do so.

After we had reached judgments about the new information, we revisited our judgments on the issues for which the new information and new insights regarding old information were germane. The estimate was rewritten and subjected, once again, to formal coordination. Given the intense interest of the Congress and the fact that we appeared likely to change one of the key judgments of the 2005 update and several previous estimates, and convinced that this estimate would be subjected to even closer scrutiny than I had anticipated when we began the project, I took the unprecedented step of asking the Analytical Integrity and Standards team that evaluated IC products to critique the draft that was submitted for coordination. The team, and to this day I do not know precisely who evaluated the draft, identified a few places requiring additional work but otherwise gave the draft high marks on all tradecraft criteria. The penultimate draft submitted for review by members of the National Intelligence Board (NIB) was approximately 140 pages long and contained nearly 1,500 source notes, all of which had been revetted a second time when we redid the estimate to incorporate new information.

Despite the generally positive reaction to the many status report briefings we provided, Congress became increasingly impatient to receive the final product. DNI Mike McConnell promised delivery by the end of November. To meet that deadline, we provided a penultimate draft to members of the National Intelligence Board so that they would be able to intervene earlier in the process than is normally the case. If we had made any errors, I wanted to know about it. And if anyone disagreed with the tentative judgments or thought that one of the "less likely" alternative explanations warranted greater prominence or a higher degree of probability, I wanted to know that. Every member of the board knew what was at stake. As noted previously, four of us had been on the board that approved the Iraq WMD estimate. We took our responsibility very seriously. Senior officials queried their own analysts and came to the table prepared for a serious discussion of every aspect of the estimate. This level of engagement and ability to wrestle with the issues in advance of the meeting was in sharp contrast to what had happened in 2002 when most of us encountered some of the intelligence and assessments of its meaning only when we arrived at what we knew would be the final meeting on the Iraq WMD estimate.

In light of the subsequent public brouhaha over the Iran nuclear NIE, it is important to set the stage by providing context for the discussion and decisions reached at the National Intelligence Board (NIB) meeting that approved the estimate. Elements of that context that I consider important include:

- Long-running discussion of how decisions to release unclassified key judgments or more extended portions of National Intelligence Estimates affected intelligence exchanges with liaison partners and whether analysts might, even subconsciously, construct their arguments and assessments differently if they thought the text would be made public. McConnell had issued guidance less than two months prior to the meeting in which he stated that it was the policy of the DNI *not* to declassify NIEs and setting out stringent criteria for doing so in exceptional circumstances.[59]
- The degree of sustained engagement by senior IC officials throughout the period in which we processed, assessed, and interpreted the new intelligence that had caused us to go back to square one and completely redo key portions of the estimate. Everyone at the table understood the sensitivity and fragility of the sources and the fact that the proposed text would change a key judgment about Iran's program that had figured prominently in the U.S. diplomatic strategy to prevent Iran from acquiring nuclear weapons.
- Most of those attending the meeting had been members of the National Intelligence Board since its inception in 2005 and had reviewed many previous NIEs. They knew, firsthand, how the introduction of new tradecraft and procedural requirements had changed and im-

proved NIEs. They had experience-based confidence in the integrity and thoroughness of the process and knew, again from experience, that the meeting was intended for serious discussion, revision of the text to enhance clarity, and final "adult supervision" of the product and how it would be presented to policy makers, foreign liaison partners, and any relevant others.

· Six members of the board currently served in positions for which they had been nominated by President Bush and confirmed by the Senate. I was the seventh Bush appointee on the board but had resigned my Senate-confirmed position as assistant secretary of state for intelligence and research to assume the deputy director of national intelligence for analysis position. This was not an "anti-Bush" cabal.[60]

It would be inappropriate to discuss what happened at the meeting in any detail, but certain aspects have already been made public and warrant repetition here. The first is that the meeting began with the explicit decision not to release an unclassified version of the estimate or its key judgments. Everyone in the room understood that we were to review and revise the text of a classified document intended to inform decisions by policy makers who knew the subject and the issues very well. We were not writing for a general audience. The second is that, as a group, we were confident that the Community had done a good job, that the evidence supported the judgments we reached, and that alternatives had been thoroughly considered in an annex to the estimate and appropriately summarized in the main text. The third is that most of the judgments presented in previous estimates on the subject were reconfirmed, in most cases with higher levels of confidence owing to the acquisition of additional information. The one very significant exception was the judgment in the 2007 estimate—based on the double-checked new intelligence streams— that Iran had halted the weaponization component of its nuclear program in 2003. The board felt that this judgment was so important that it should be the lead sentence and that it should be followed immediately by the companion judgment that, at a minimum, Tehran was keeping open the option to develop nuclear weapons.[61] Giving prominence to the judgment that had changed was also consistent with the requirement spelled out in *Intelligence Community Directive 203: Analytic Standards.*

The NIB recommended approval of the estimate, with specified changes to the key judgments, and the final version was delivered to the executive branch and the Congress on December 1. Weeks before the estimate was finalized, senior officials in both branches were told that most key judgments from pre-vious estimates would be reaffirmed in the new one but that the IC might change its judgment on whether Iran was driving to acquire a nuclear weapon as quickly as possible or had suspended work on the weaponization portion of the program. Not very many officials in either branch were told this, but all who were briefed were told the same thing. The judgments of the IC did not become final until the DNI accepted the recommendation of the National Intelligence Board.

Although the estimate had been drafted with the strong expectation that it would remain a classified document, the White House determined that the key judgments should—and would—be declassified and released. It is my un-derstanding that there were two reasons for doing so. One can be summarized as "because it is the right thing to do." For years, the United States had used Intelligence Community judgments about Iran's nuclear ambitions and capa-bilities to persuade other nations of the need for concerted diplomatic action to prevent Tehran from acquiring the bomb. Having done so, it was argued, we had an obligation to tell others that the IC had changed its assessment re-garding one of the key aspects of Iran's program. The second, and more often cited, reason was concern that the altered key judgment would leak and that its interpretation would be distorted if it were not put in the context of the other judgments contained in the estimate. To get out in front of distorting leaks, as much of the original key judgments section of the estimate was to be declassified as could be done without endangering sources and methods or diplomatic relations with U.S. partners and without telling Iranians more than we wanted to about what we did and did not know about their program.[62]

Preparation of the unclassified version of the key judgments was guided by clear instructions from the White House to delete as little as possible and by the criteria prescribed by the internal guidance that Mike McConnell had issued just weeks before.[63] That guidance was intended both to limit the number of times key judgments would be declassified and to avoid repetition of the dis-tortions and confusion engendered by the unclassified White Paper on Iraq's WMD programs that was released at almost the same time that the classified NIE on that subject was delivered to the executive branch and the Congress. The newly issued guidelines can be summarized as requiring that the declassi-fied version fully and accurately mirror the classified version except for the ex-cisions needed to protect sources and to satisfy the other enumerated criteria.

The decision to release an unclassified version of the key judgments meant that both the Intelligence Community and the policy community had to revise what Washington jargon refers to as the "rollout strategy" for the Iran nuclear estimate. For the IC, this typically requires the preparation of two or three classified versions of an estimate that can be shared with allies and liaison partners. These revised or redacted versions are prepared in accordance with the nature of our intelligence-sharing relationships with different categories of liaison partners. Each must accurately reflect the key judgments, but they differ with regard to the amount and character of the supporting information provided. With plans to release the unclassified version on December 3, a Monday (in Washington, it seems always to be the case that such undertakings have to be completed over the weekend), we had to accelerate plans to brief our partners so that they would not first learn of our judgments via the media.

The State Department was supposed to conduct a parallel set of briefings highlighting the NIE's higher level of confidence that Iran had conducted a secret program; had lied about the program to the International Atomic Energy Agency, the U.N. Security Council, and the so-called EU-3 negotiators (the United Kingdom, France, and Germany); and was still capable of producing enough highly enriched uranium for a nuclear device within the same time frame (possibly but unlikely by late 2009, more likely in the first half of the next decade) as had been assessed in previous estimates. A critical point that I certainly expected to be made in the policy rollout was that even though the Intelligence Community now assessed that Iran had halted the weaponization program in 2003, it had not changed the time line for when Iran would be capable of producing enough highly enriched uranium for a nuclear device. This was the pacing element of Iran's program, not how long it would take to construct a workable device once it had enough highly enriched uranium. I also expected the diplomatic strategy to emphasize that the IC judged that Iran was keeping open the option to pursue a weapon and that the weaponization component of the program could be restarted at any time if the Iranians decided to do so. Finally, I anticipated that the diplomatic strategy would emphasize the judgment of the NIE that international scrutiny and pressure (not further specified) had caused Tehran to suspend at least the weaponization portion of its secret program. In other words, diplomacy had worked and could work again. For reasons unknown to me, the policy component of the rollout strategy was not fully implemented.

The Intelligence Community rollout entailed offers to brief members of Congress and a briefing for the media. Principal Deputy Director of National Intelligence Don Kerr headed the media briefing. DNI McConnell would have chaired the session, but he had departed on a previously scheduled trip. The other briefers were Director of Central Intelligence Mike Hayden; myself, as the chairman of the National Intelligence Council; and National Intelligence Officer for Weapons of Mass Destruction Vann Van Diepen. Kerr, Van Diepen, and I were there by virtue of our formal positions and roles in the preparation of the NIE; Hayden requested to be at the table because of the role that CIA analysts had played in the process.

The IC press briefing occurred on December 3, and articles began to appear the same day. Although the stories that I read and heard were accurate with respect to what the unclassified key judgments said, and what they meant, many of them also juxtaposed the judgments of the IC and statements made previously by members of the administration.[64] For the next several months, spin and fantasy displaced serious discussion of the NIE's findings or tradecraft, and at times I had a sense that I was moving among several parallel universes. Before examining some of the zanier subplots in the tale, I must note that my expectation that the estimate and its tradecraft would be examined closely and that close scrutiny would reveal how lessons from the Iraq WMD estimate had been implemented and how doing so had improved the quality and clarity of IC analysis proved to be completely wrong, at least in the short run.

The opening shot at the NIE was a *Wall Street Journal* editorial published on December 5 that decries the sorry state of the Intelligence Community, disparages the Bush administration, and characterizes the estimate as the work of "hyper-partisan anti-Bush officials" Fingar, Van Diepen, and head of the National Counter-Proliferation Center Ken Brill.[65] Employing much of the same language, John Bolton published an op ed on December 6 that correctly noted little substantive difference between the conclusions of the 2005 update and the 2007 NIE but disparaged the possibility that Iran might be susceptible to diplomatic persuasion and dismissed the NIE itself as nothing more than a political polemic ascribed to "refugees from the State Department" (presumably Fingar, Van Diepen, and Brill) who, he claimed, were not intelligence professionals.[66]

These dismissals of the estimate on what amounted to spurious ad hominem grounds were repeated over and over again in conservative media. For the record, none of us were "main authors" of the estimate—senior, career analysts from the line intelligence agencies were. As a matter of policy, the Intelligence Community does not reveal publicly the names of the analysts who have drafted or contributed to the production of NIEs. The responsible NIO (or occasionally a deputy NIO) and the chairman of the NIC provide the public face and take the heat or get the credit when briefing on the Hill. Also for the record, I had been in the Intelligence Community for thirty-seven years at that point. There was a great deal of mindless mimicry and an astounding lack of effort to check assertions, but those who disagreed with the judgment that Iran might be susceptible to diplomacy appear to have had a clear and effective strategy intended to deflect attention away from serious discussion of whether or under what conditions diplomacy might be effective by focusing on the alleged incompetence or political agendas of putative authors.

Conservative ideologues were not the only ones who embraced ad hominem arguments, however. Google sent me links to dozens of media pieces published in the days after release of the Iran estimate, and the ones praising my heroism for allegedly thwarting the president's intention to invade Iran are as goofy and erroneous as the ones painting me as a villain.[67] Media accounts are what they are, and most should not be taken seriously were it not for the fact that they shape the views of the American public and, more importantly, members of Congress. Nevertheless, I found the commentaries less troubling than some of the reactions I encountered on the Hill.

In the weeks after release of the Iran NIE, I briefed our findings to several committees and individual members. Van Diepen and others on the NIC briefed many others. After the first of these briefings, one of the members reached across the table, took my hand, and said, "Thank you for your courage and integrity. The American people owe you a debt of gratitude." I did not know whether he meant me personally or intended "you" to be a collective noun embracing all who had worked on the NIE but hoped it was the latter. The first time, the comment was gratifying, but it was repeated, with only slight variations, after almost every briefing and came from members of both parties and in both houses. Each repetition left me more discomforted because the statements implied that integrity was rare and heroic when I believe that it is the coin of the realm in the Intelligence Community. If we lack or are not seen to have integrity, we are little more than a useless waste of taxpayer money. Despite all the effort and all the progress that I believe we had made to improve the quality of analytic products, even those who "liked" our conclusions often attributed them to personality rather than professionalism. I did and still do find this very disappointing.[68]

THE REST OF THE STORY

This tale has many more subplots that are probably worthy of exploration but are better reserved for another time and a different venue. Some of them do, however, warrant brief mention before bringing this part of the story to a close. The most important part of the continuing saga concerns the success of efforts to learn and apply lessons from the Iraq WMD case to achieve continuous improvement and enhanced understanding of Intelligence Community assessments. I feel quite good about what we achieved during the time that I headed the drive to transform analysis in the IC and am confident that the changes we made are producing demonstrable improvement and restoring confidence in our people and our analysis of complex issues. The strong tradecraft of the Iran Nuclear NIE was overshadowed by partisan politics and preoccupation with other issues and did not have the demonstration effect that I hoped and expected it to have.

In retrospect, however, I may have expected too much and looked for the wrong indicator of success. Washington can be a very tough town, and I probably should have been attentive to the dogs that did not bark. Although the estimate did not garner the explicit praise that I hoped it would, neither did it evoke serious or specific criticism (except from those who thought we should have written the key judgments in a way that would make them easily understandable to members of the public). Over time, people with the required clearances did look closely at the estimate. They found much to commend, in private, and nothing to justify another round of public criticism. In Washington, criticism of shortcomings is far more common than is praise of accomplishment. In the case of the Iran nuclear estimate, the paucity of serious criticism and absence of public excoriation is tantamount to praise because to visibly praise something is to invite ridicule in the future if the reformed drunk falls off the wagon or the transformed Intelligence Community produces another high-profile product with consequential defects. It is politically safer to quietly pat the Community on the head in a closed or private setting.

7 EPILOGUE

Lessons and Challenges

PRECEDING CHAPTERS HAVE discussed what intelligence analysts do to reduce uncertainty about places, people, and problems of interest to national security decision makers. The discussion was largely descriptive and analytic because my primary objective was to convey a sense of how analysis fits into the broader intelligence enterprise by exploring what intelligence customers want, need, and expect from the analysts who support them and what it is like to work in the fast-paced, highly consequential, and often politically charged atmosphere in Washington. As noted in Chapter 1, I have eschewed feigned objectivity because I want readers, especially those currently serving as intelligence analysts, to understand how the intelligence enterprise looks to a long-serving analyst who made it to the top of our profession and was given the opportunity to formulate and implement IC-wide efforts to improve analytic performance.

I am confident that others with long service in the Intelligence Community share many of the observations and judgments presented in this volume, but I am also certain that none will concur with all of them. My interpretation of what analysts do is not inherently better or worse than was the description of the elephant offered by each of the blind men; like them, I and every other commentator on the intelligence enterprise must extrapolate from personal experience and partial information. My perspective is shaped by nearly four decades of work in or for the Intelligence Community, more than half of which was in senior positions.

Many of my observations about the intelligence enterprise result from the self-imposed requirement to think systematically and critically about the roles and responsibilities of intelligence analysts induced by the momentary panic that ensued when I realized the scope, requirements, and potential implications of what I had committed to do when I agreed to serve as the first deputy director of national intelligence for analysis (DDNI/A).[1] My mandate—and commitment—was to "fix" IC analysis in ways that would preclude repetition of the shortcomings, errors, and problems identified by the 9/11 Commission, the Senate Select Committee on Intelligence, the WMD Commission, and myriad other critics inspired and emboldened by the tragic events of September 11, 2001, and the flawed estimate on Iraq's weapons of mass destruction.[2] The magnitude of that commitment was underscored the day after I accepted the assignment when my new boss, newly confirmed Director of National Intelligence John Negroponte, opened the conversation in his temporary office in the Old Executive Office Building by saying, "Thanks for accepting this assignment. What are you going to do?"

I do not remember precisely what I said in response, but it amounted to "I don't know yet but will get back to you as soon as I get my arms around the problem." The effort to do so entailed reflection about change and continuities in the missions and structure of the Intelligence Community, what had worked relatively well or badly in the past, and myriad similar questions. That effort continued throughout my tenure as DDNI/A. It was very much an iterative process in which tentative conclusions about the current state and future requirements of the Intelligence Community (IC) shaped initial steps to implement mandated or desirable changes, and evaluation of what happened in the course of implementation led to refined—or entirely new—judgments about the IC and its relationship to policy makers. The process continues.

A second reason for writing this book is to enhance public understanding of what intelligence analysts do and how and why we do it. The Intelligence Community expends a great deal of money to reduce uncertainty about threats to the security of our nation, the safety of our people, and the success of our foreign policies, but mythology and misinformation have created a very distorted picture of what IC analysts can (and cannot) do. Among other consequences, this reduces public—and congressional—confidence in the Intelligence Community and the measures adopted to protect our nation. This book endeavors to clarify the nature of the mission and to increase confidence in the capabilities of intelligence analysts while at the same time trying to put reasonable bounds on expectations about what we can do. Better understanding of the capabilities and limitations of intelligence should lead to reassessment of strategies for managing and mitigating several kinds of risks.

Enhanced understanding of what intelligence analysts do may also improve the utility of proposals to enhance IC analytic performance and accelerate the process of analytic transformation needed to meet the challenges of today and tomorrow. Having led the process for four years, I know well both the magnitude of the challenges and the inadequacy of what has been accomplished to date. The IC analytic community has made a good start, but far more needs to be done, and it needs to be done as quickly as possible. To date, the effort has been hobbled by the paucity of well-grounded suggestions from outside the Intelligence Community and the need to divert time and effort to deflecting unhelpful and counterproductive proposals. Better understanding of what we actually do should improve the relevance and utility of external proposals. One can never have too many good ideas, but we now spend too much time beating back bad ideas and too little exploring or testing ideas that might make a positive difference.

To stimulate and focus additional suggestions for improving intelligence analysis, I will close with brief descriptions of four overarching challenges that must be addressed in the years ahead. Each of the challenges reflects lessons learned from my own iterative examination of what the Intelligence Community does and what intelligence analysts must do to meet rapidly changing demands for information and insight. The list could easily be expanded, but doing so risks diluting the importance of the challenges that I regard as critical to the attainment of numerous other goals.

WORKING SMARTER

Intelligence analysts are expected to do more things better and more quickly today than ever before. Previous generations of analysts have made the same observation, often accompanied by pleas for "more" intelligence and, later, for better ways to manage and manipulate data accumulating more quickly than it could be examined. Responses to their complaints and appeals for help generally evolved as follows: Collectors received more money and more tools to collect more information, and analysts were told to work harder. Sooner or later, there was a breakdown or "intelligence failure" that triggered the traditional fix of adding more money and more people to the intelligence budget. In more recent times, it also included purchasing more computers and software that never lived up to what was promised. Though far from elegant or efficient, this general approach and pattern of developments worked well enough to forestall serious efforts to transform the intelligence process and the way analysts do their jobs.[3]

At the end of each round of this repetitive cycle, analysts made a little headway in coping with new demands and increased volumes of intelligence, but by and large they continued to do what they had always done in more or less the same ways that they had always done it. For a long time, that approach was good enough, or so it seemed until the next breakdown or failure restarted the cycle. But what worked well enough in the past is no longer adequate and will be increasingly inadequate in the future. Developments summarized in previous chapters underscore the need for fundamental change; the aftermath of the 9/11 and the Iraq WMD estimate "failures" created an unprecedented opportunity to revamp—transform—the intelligence enterprise. We must seize that opportunity because throwing more money and more people at the problem and "working harder" will not be adequate. We have to work smarter.

Working smarter has several dimensions, including more—and more productive—collaboration with persons inside and outside the Intelligence Community (see the following discussion), doing more to ensure that IC analytic efforts focus on dimensions of issues and developments that are most important to customers in the policy community and/or will give them the most or best insight into the issues they are working (also discussed in the following pages), and seeking continuous improvement through rigorous evaluation of performance and systematic application of lessons learned from the evaluative process. The last of these suggestions should not be construed as implying that current practices and performance are badly deficient (I believe that they are not, but such a judgment should be based on empirical data, not faith and subjectivity). However, even the best of current practices can be improved. More to the point, they must improve if IC analysts are to keep pace with escalating demands and expectations.

The evaluation of analytic products using tradecraft standards incorporated into *Intelligence Community Directive (ICD) 203: Analytic Standards* and *ICD 206: Sourcing Requirements for Disseminated Analytic Products* is a good start in the right direction, but much more can and should be done on a routine basis.[4] Illustrative examples of other products, techniques, and procedures that can and should be evaluated continuously include the efficacy (relative and absolute) of the hundred or more analytic methods and tools used by IC analysts; the utility, value, and (when appropriate) accuracy of assessments of particular subjects by analysts in different components of the IC; the performance of individual analysts, formal teams, and virtual teams collaborating in A-Space or other cyberworkspaces; and how systematically analysts and teams apply tradecraft methods throughout the analytic process. Each of these topics warrants brief elaboration.

IC analysts utilize an enormous range of methods, techniques, and tools when formulating research questions, developing strategies to answer those questions, assessing and interpreting data, and employing assumptions and analogies to bridge information gaps.[5] Much of what they do, much of the time, is a mix of skills learned in graduate school, formal training and mentoring after joining the Intelligence Community, "new" methods introduced by colleagues or vendors, and suggestions or instructions from supervisors. Individual analysts use what is familiar, what seemed to work in the past (however that was determined), or what seems most appropriate to a specific situation (however determined). Increased attention to the basic tradecraft standards specified in relevant ICDs has made some portions of the process somewhat more rigorous, but, by and large, analysts do not have an empirical basis for using or eschewing particular methods.

A second area ripe for evaluation is the value of analytic products generated and disseminated by different elements of the IC. The Community produces thousands—tens of thousands—of analytic pieces every year, and there is a great deal of redundancy in the coverage of specific topics and developments. Some redundancy is more apparent than real. For example, multiple agencies may write on the same subject within a short period but examine quite different dimensions of the subject because they are targeted at different customers. This is good and reflects the premium that customers attach to tailored support from the Intelligence Community. In other cases—how many remains to be determined—redundant analyses are truly duplicative, citing the same evidence and reaching the same conclusions. The first question that should be asked when this happens is, "Why did agency X produce and disseminate its own assessment when it could have used a product from another agency?" Similarly, it seems likely that all agencies do better work on some subjects than on others, and that some of what they do is systematically better or worse than comparable work done elsewhere. Evaluations to determine such strengths and weaknesses and feedback and learning mechanisms to capitalize on strengths and take appropriate action with respect to weaknesses would be extremely helpful for raising overall performance, reducing duplication, and ensuring that all customers who need it get access to the best analysis available.

Another area ripe for evaluation is the performance of individual analysts and analyst teams. The priority objective should be to determine under what circumstances individual effort, persistent teams of persons in the same agency, ad hoc groupings within or across agency boundaries, and different types of "virtual teams" working in cyberspace perform most effectively, not which analyst or team is "best" or "worst." Analysts work in many different ways (for many different reasons), but we lack an empirical basis to determine which ways are best in general and/or for the analysis of particular types of problems under different time constraints and so on. We could know this, and we should know this. What we discover should be fed back into training programs, mentoring arrangements, and guidance to analytic supervisors.

The last illustrative example of behaviors that can and should be evaluated centers on what analysts actually do when defining and prioritizing the questions they intend to examine; how they search for relevant information ("raw" intelligence, previously published IC analytic pieces on the subject, "open source" publications, others thought to have relevant expertise, and so on); how they determine what approach, methodology, or tools to use; how they actually apply the chosen methods; and similar questions. One goal of determining what analysts actually do (and do not do) is to develop efficient and effective procedures that can be taught and monitored across the Community. They might even lead to the production of "checklists" of the kind used by airline pilots and some medical specialists. These techniques have been shown to improve performance in other demanding professions and might well be helpful in the IC analytic community.

COLLABORATION

Contemporary intelligence problems are too complex, too fast moving, and too information rich to be analyzed by individuals or, much of the time, individual agencies. Individual analysts, no matter how smart, experienced, or heroic, cannot hope to monitor *all* intelligence germane to their accounts or to possess *all* the disciplinary, regional, and technical knowledge required to answer the kinds of questions routinely directed to the Intelligence Community. To paraphrase the Beatles, the only way to provide satisfactory support to demanding customers with consequential responsibilities is to seek and accept more than a little help from friends and colleagues. Collaboration is not a luxury or "nice to do" way to do analysis; it may be the only acceptable way to do it in a large and growing number of cases.

Intelligence veterans point out, correctly, that collaboration is not a new idea or requirement; agencies and analysts have always worked together to solve hard problems and produce coordinated assessments. This observation is correct, but the frequency, forms, and necessity of collaboration are substantially different than in the past. Indeed, for much of my career, ways in which IC components worked together were described as forms of cooperation or coordination, not collaboration. The difference is subtle but important. Cooperation in the IC often had a reluctant or coerced character—analysts were asked or forced to cooperate on something but would have preferred sole ownership of the task. Similarly, when agencies were required to coordinate or cooperate on a specific product, like a National Intelligence Estimate or Congressional testimony, the process was often likened to what the Chinese Communist Party used to refer to as "struggle sessions."

Among the reasons that cooperation was often grudging, at best, was that the requirement for "competitive analysis" had mutated into a perverse desire to scoop the competition in ways reminiscent of the late-nineteenth- and early-twentieth-century newspaper wars between the Hearst and Pulitzer papers.[6] Individuals and agencies often strove to get "their" take on new developments or new intelligence to policy makers before their "competitors" elsewhere in the IC. This perversion put a higher premium on being first than on being right, a situation that I often characterized as the quest to be the first to misinform senior decision makers. The consequences of this interpretation of competitive analysis included analytical work that was not as good as it could or should have been and instances in which policy makers became vested in erroneous judgments before the IC had a chance to correct them.

Collaboration, in contrast to grudging cooperation or coordination, should—must—be a willing combination of institutional linkages that take advantage of divisions of labor and inherent opportunities for synergy and bottom-up pooling of expertise. The legacy structure—and the logic of specialization that spawned the multiplicity of analytic units in the Intelligence Community—is a mixed blessing for collaboration. The attribute that has been most criticized and is, in fact, the greatest impediment to analytic collaboration is the existence of excessively independent organizations that have been characterized as "stove-piped feudal baronies" disinterested in collaboration and seeking to monopolize contacts between "their" customers and the IC as a whole.[7] The criticisms are exaggerated but contain more than a grain of truth. The resultant clashes of culture and mutual rivalries have been significant impediments to the sharing of information, sensible divisions of labor, and collaboration of other kinds. These pathologies are not as bad as they were, but we still have a long way to go to surmount them.

The flip side of the existing structure is that it has fostered development of different types of expertise to support different missions and customers. As a result, the aggregation of analytic organizations has tremendous breadth, less duplication than many contend, and inherent complementarities that can be harnessed to establish formal and informal divisions of labor and to aggregate individual expertise to achieve the critical mass and complementarities needed to understand complex issues. Realizing the potential inherent in the structure of the Community is an important goal of analytic transformation and requires integrated progress on multiple dimensions. How to do this is the subject of a future book on analytic transformation; the point I want to make here is that creating and capitalizing on conditions conducive to collaboration is one of the most pressing challenges facing the analytic community.

One additional attribute of the existing structure warrants attention here, namely, that it entails both necessary and unnecessary duplication. Necessary duplication is the result of the fact that multiple individual and institutional IC customers work the same or overlapping issues. For example, decision makers in the State Department, the Pentagon, and at Treasury all require IC support on China, the Middle East, and Africa, but the specific issues in each country and region that they are interested in are different, and so too must be the expertise of the intelligence analysts who support them. The result is necessary duplication at one level (for example, specific countries) but complementarities with respect to the dimensions of the country (for example, politics, military developments, or trade) of most concern to particular customers. As a result, the IC structure ensures multiple independent perspectives on a wide array of issues and facilitates acquisition of "second opinions" and "alternative assessments." This type of duplication is essential and must be preserved. Unnecessary duplication also exists because of bureaucratic rivalry, understandable but unfortunate pursuit of analytic autarky, and ignorance of capabilities in other components of the IC. With greater transparency and trust in the capabilities and responsiveness of IC colleagues, it should be possible to reduce the amount of unnecessary duplication in a way that strengthens groups that are best at a particular set of tasks, eliminates those that are weakest with respect to those tasks, and preserves at least two clusters of expertise on all subjects so that the IC never has a single point of failure or single take on any issue of importance.

Collaboration must occur in multiple and overlapping "arenas" (that is, within agencies, across agency boundaries, among IC analysts and USG decision makers, and among IC analysts and experts outside of government and, in many cases, outside the United States).[8] The aphorism "two heads are better than one" certainly pertains, as do variants such as "analysts from multiple agencies often are better than analysts from a single agency" and "analysts with multiple perspectives are better than analysts with the same perspective." Even without formal divisions of labor, analysts in one part of the Intelligence Community tend to look at different kinds of information than do counterparts in other components, and they tend to look for answers to different kinds of questions. Collaboration facilitates more comprehensive and more nuanced assessments, but it also helps ensure that customers in different parts of the policy community understand the information and analytic input being provided to colleagues elsewhere in the USG. In other words, collaboration can produce both better analysis and better intelligence support to customers across the USG.

Effective and efficient collaboration within the Intelligence Community requires easy access to the same information. This does not mean that all analysts working a problem must receive the same intelligence, but it does mean that it must be easy for colleagues to share information and insights derived from intelligence with colleagues in other components of the IC. Innovations such as A-Space and the Library of National Intelligence have made it much easier for IC analysts to share information and collaborate in cyberspace, but similar mechanisms (and supporting policy guidance) are needed to facilitate comparable forms of collaboration with USG experts outside the Intelligence Community and specialists in academe, think tanks, and other nongovernment institutions.

In my experience, analysts, especially younger analysts, are strongly predisposed to collaborate and very comfortable working in virtual teams and cyberspace. This predisposition creates unprecedented opportunities for collaboration across time and space, the production of "living documents" that belong to the IC as a whole rather than to one analyst or agency, and dramatic reduction of the number of analytic products. To the extent that analysts collaborate and produce joint products that can be used by multiple agencies to support many different customers, the IC will be able to reduce the number of separate documents disseminated to customers, and the documents they do provide will be better than the sum of numerous separate products.

TRUST AND CONFIDENCE

Collaboration among analysts requires confidence in one another and in the quality of the work done by colleagues working in different components of the IC. The former requires overcoming negative stereotypes and disparaging characterizations of analysts in other agencies. Negative characterizations are engendered by misguided efforts to build esprit de corps in one agency by denigrating the people and practices of other components and by lack of information about the background, responsibilities, and tradecraft of the people who contribute to unsigned publications. The structure of the IC facilitates collaboration through the development of complementary areas of expertise but impedes it by creating cultural differences and bureaucratic rivalries.

Several measures have been adopted to mitigate such impediments to collaboration, including joint training in analytic tradecraft (intended to build confidence in the work performed elsewhere in the IC by demonstrating that analysts from all agencies have more or less the same backgrounds and abilities and have received the same training with regard to the use of intelligence in analytic products). Absent confidence in the people and the quality of their work, it is impossible to implement divisions of labor or to use work prepared elsewhere in the IC to answer requests from customers. We have made progress toward overcoming confidence-related impediments to collaboration but still have far to go even within the IC.

The situation with respect to the confidence that customers have in the analytic community is even more problematic. One aspect of the problem reflects the tendency of people to have more confidence in those they know than in those they have never met. As customers get to know their own intelligence support team and to calibrate the quality and utility of the intelligence it provides, they tend to evaluate analysis on the basis of who provided it rather than on its inherent value. Such a tendency has been exacerbated by the perverse interpretation of "competitive analysis" and attendant tendency of many analysts to inflate the quality and importance of their own work by criticizing the work of colleagues. One consequence is that analysts supporting a particular customer have to do more work because their customer does not want to settle for work prepared in another agency.

Trust is about more than just the quality of analytic products. To provide timely and targeted intelligence support, analysts need to know what customers are working on, are worried about, and hope to accomplish. They also need to know what the customer knows (or thinks he or she knows) about the subject and what that customer wants to know. Analysts are able to be helpful to decision makers in direct proportion to how much they know about what officials think and how they are trying to work a problem. The less they know, the more likely they are to miss the mark when preparing or delivering intelligence products. But to be that knowledgeable about the goals and needs of policy makers entails risks of politicization and cooptation. Every analyst must win the trust of primary customers without violating ethical and professional standards. Sometimes that can be difficult to do.

TRANSFORMING THE INTELLIGENCE COMMUNITY

IC analysts, especially those who have joined the Intelligence Community in the years since 9/11, are excited by the challenges described in this volume and eager to tear down, overcome, or end-run impediments to doing all that they can to reduce uncertainty and protect our nation. Many embrace the philosophy of life reflected in the Army recruiting appeal to "be all that you can be" and the Nike slogan "Just do it" and seek to apply that philosophy in their professional lives. They want to do high-quality analytic work, want to make meaningful contributions to national security, and aspire to "make a difference" through public service. They are well educated, often well traveled, and digitally savvy. The digital generation is also the generation of Google, Facebook, and Twitter.

Collaboration in cyberspace with little—or no—regard for bureaucratic or other boundaries is as natural as breathing to most younger analysts and, contrary to what one might expect, to many veteran analysts as well. In short, the analytic workforce is ready and eager for transformative changes that will unleash their potential and allow them to operate in their professional environment the way they operated in graduate school and do things outside of work. When, and to the extent, changes made under the rubric of analytic transformation increase latitude for bottom-up change, analysts embrace the opportunity and invent new ways to communicate and collaborate. It would be difficult to imagine a more propitious set of circumstances for effecting the transformative changes required to keep pace with demands and developments. The analysts are ready to go.

Analytic transformation has made great strides during the past five years, but most steps have been slower and more painful than they should have been. Veterans understand that change is difficult, especially when it challenges or undermines long-standing procedures and bureaucratic fiefdoms, and they counsel patience. But another characteristic of our younger analysts is that they are impatient. Youth have always been impatient, but, perhaps more than was the case with any preceding generation, impatience is now compounded by expectations of frequent movement among public, private, and nonprofit jobs. If impatience morphs into frustration, many will vote with their feet and move on to something different sooner than might otherwise be the case. This poses a double challenge to Intelligence Community managers. Not only must they work harder than in the past to retain analysts for longer periods than predictions indicate will be normal for newer recruits to avoid the perils of rapid and extensive turnover just at the point when analysts have become sufficiently experienced to begin making solid and sustained contributions, they must also prevent large numbers from leaving earlier than they otherwise would because of frustration over what they regard as unnecessary impediments to high performance and professional growth. The severe economic downturn in 2008–2009 probably gave the Intelligence Community more time than it otherwise would have had to "fix" problems that frustrate analysts eager for rapid and radical change, but there is a danger that retention attributable to the bad economy has created pent-up potential for departures when the economy improves.

Retention is an important issue and adds urgency to the need for transformative change, but the primary reason for accelerating transformation is—and should be—to enhance the ability of analysts to reduce uncertainty by providing more accurate, more insightful, and more precisely focused support to national decision makers. Indeed, this is actually a "twofer" because making it easier for analysts to do quality work also increases the likelihood of professional satisfaction and decisions by analysts to remain in the Intelligence Community. Analysts can do and have done a lot to unleash their potential and address the growing and changing challenges they confront, but IC analysts are embedded in the broader intelligence enterprise, and changes to a number of policies and procedures that affect what analysts can do must be tackled at the enterprise level. Stated differently, there are limits to change that can be achieved from the bottom up; complementary and enabling changes must be made from the top down.

Establishment of the Office of the Director of National Intelligence (ODNI) in December 2004 improved prospects for top-down changes to integrate the Intelligence Community and ameliorate pathological consequences resulting from its federated structure and the independent and autarkical behaviors that emerged and became entrenched because directors of central intelligence lacked the authority, incentives, or time to transform members of the notional "community" into a single integrated enterprise with specialized components. Many responsibilities were assigned to the director of national intelligence by the Intelligence Reform and Terrorism Prevention Act of December 2004, but none is more important, in my view, than the mandate to integrate the IC.[9]

Integration of the IC has proven to be more difficult than appears to have been expected by advocates of creating the ODNI and members of Congress responsible for intelligence oversight. One can point to a number of reasons to account for the difficulty, including expectations and aspirations that the ODNI "experiment" would fail and things would revert to the way they were prior to 2005; concern on the part of customers served by in-house or dedicated intelligence units (for example, those embedded in the State Department, the Department of Energy, Treasury, and those supporting each of the military services) that integration would deprive them of the dedicated, tailored, and proximate intelligence support they considered essential to perform their missions; and concern on the part of many that effective integration would spell the end of "competitive analysis," alternative judgments, and second opinions on critical issues, leading to groupthink and domination by a single big agency with the initials CIA.

I was on record (in my June 2004 confirmation hearing for the position of INR assistant secretary) as opposing creation of the Office of the Director of National Intelligence. At the time, I viewed questions about the desirability of creating a director of national intelligence posed to me by Senator Lugar through the lens of my intelligence unit and our responsibilities to support the secretary of state and diplomatic missions around the world and saw a strong DNI as a threat to INR's ability to perform its critical but largely niche mission of support to diplomacy.[10] Moreover, given INR's long history of dissent from consensus judgments of the Intelligence Community, I also worried about the perils of groupthink and big agency dominance. The lessons of the Iraq WMD estimate were very much on my mind. Having opposed creation of the ODNI, I suppose that it was somehow appropriate that I should have been tapped as the first deputy DNI for analysis because others could be reasonably confident that I would not attempt to dismantle or derail what I regarded as great strengths and essential attributes of the then extant Intelligence Community. In the years since, I have become convinced that the existence and exercise of DNI authorities are absolutely essential to transforming the Intelligence Community, and that transforming the Community as a whole is essential for transforming the analytic community in ways that will enable it to meet twenty-first-century challenges and expectations.

Unless we continue to integrate the IC and to evaluate and improve the way analysts do their jobs, we will not be able to do all that we can and must do to reduce uncertainty about issues affecting national security. As a congenital optimist, I believe that we will do so and that the American people will continue to reap the benefits they expect and deserve from their intelligence analysts.

REFERENCE MATTER

NOTES

Chapter 1

1. Financial Year 2010 NOAA Budget Highlights, Weather (National Weather Service) at www.corporateservices.noaa.gov/nbo/FY10_BlueBook/NWS_OnePager_050609.pdf.

2. Fiscal Year 2010 Budget in Brief, Centers for Disease Control and Prevention at www.hhs.gov/asrt/ob/docbudget/2010budgetinbriefg.html.

3. See, for example, U.S. Department of Agriculture, World Agricultural Supply and Demand Estimates, at www.usda.gov/oce/commodity/wasde/latest.pdf; and U.S. Energy Information Administration, Annual Energy Outlook Early Release Overview, Report No. DOE/EIA-0383 (2009), December 14, 2009, at www.eia.doe.gov/oiaf/aeo/overview.html.

4. Office of the Director of National Intelligence, "DNI Releases Budget Figure for 2010 National Intelligence Program," October 28, 2010, at www.dni.gov/press_releases/20101028_2010_NIP_release.pdf.

5. See, for example, Dennis C. Blair, director of national intelligence, Annual Threat Assessment of the US Intelligence Community for the Senate Select Committee on Intelligence, February 2, 2010, at www.dni.gov/testimonies/20100202_testimony.pdf.

6. This point is discussed at greater length in Chapter 4.

7. This is not to suggest that scholars, journalists, bankers, diplomats, or many others who routinely ask questions and gather information are "spies." "Spies" use clandestine or covert means to obtain information; the others cited here are what is known in the jargon of intelligence as "overt collectors," and the information they collect and disseminate is referred to as "open-source intelligence" in Washington's arcane way of referring to ordinary information.

8. Carl Ford held a number of senior positions in the Intelligence Community, including assistant secretary for intelligence and research, policy positions in the Department of Defense, and staff positions on the Hill.

9. Some readers may have heard me say in other contexts that my own estimate of IC performance puts our batting average at somewhere around .850—far higher than necessary to gain admission to the Hall of Fame—but that I would actually like to see our batting average go down somewhat. The reason, as I made clear in the talks, is that such a high average when we exist to tackle hard questions on which there is scant information suggests that we are spending too much effort on questions that are easy, just to inflate our average. The serious point here is that the IC should focus on the most difficult questions to the extent that answering such questions will enhance understanding and reduce uncertainty about issues that really matter. We are likely to be partially wrong more often if we do this, but the potential benefits to those we serve are likely to be greater than they are from simply increasing their comfort level with regard to things they already think they understand well enough to make decisions. Doing this would be difficult because those we support would not want to pay the opportunity cost.

10. These and other "tradecraft" requirements are spelled out in *Intelligence Community Directive 203: Analytic Standards* (ICD 203), June 21, 2007, at www.dni.gov/ electronic_reading_room/ICD_203.pdf; *Intelligence Community Directive 206: Sourcing Requirements for Disseminated Products* (ICD 206), October 17, 2007, at www .dni.gov/electronic_reading_room/ICD_206.pdf; and *Intelligence Community Directive 208: Write for Maximum Utility* (ICD 208), December 17, 2008, at www.dni.gov/ electronic_reading_room/ICD_208.pdf.

11. How one determines the "right" questions to ask; when relevant information, insights, and answers are needed to inform decisions; and who needs the information (that is, which officials in addition to the immediate customers of the analysts working the problem need the information because they also will be part of the decision making process) are themes addressed in all chapters of this book. See also Thomas Fingar, "Analysis in the US Intelligence Community: Missions, Masters, and Methods," B. Fischoff and C. Chauvin, editors, *Intelligence Analysis: Behavioral and Social Scientific Foundations* (Washington, DC: The National Academies Press, 2011), Chapter 1; and Thomas Fingar, "Office of the Director of National Intelligence: Promising Start Despite Ambiguity, Ambivalence, and Animosity," in Roger Z. George and Harvey Rishikof, eds., *The National Security Enterprise: Navigating the Labyrinth* (Washington, DC: Georgetown University Press, 2011), 139–155.

12. On the challenges of efforts to deny information and deceive observers see, for example, James B. Bruce and Michael Bennet, "Foreign Denial and Deception: Analytical Imperatives," in Roger Z. George and James B. Bruce, eds., *Analyzing Intel-*

ligence: Origins, Obstacles, and Innovations (Washington, DC: Georgetown University Press, 2008), 122–137.

13. For an example of actions taken in response to flawed intelligence analysis, see James Risen, "To Bomb Sudan Plant, or Not: A Year Later, Debates Rankle," *New York Times*, October 27, 1999, at: http://web.archive.org/web/20000831005711/http://www.library.cornell.edu/colldev/mideast/sudbous.htm.

14. See, for example, Ellen Laipson, "Think Tanks: Supporting Cast Players in the National Security Enterprise," in George and Rishikof (2011), 289–299; and Gerald Felix Warburg, "Lobbyists: U.S. National Security and Special Interests," in George and Rishikof (2011), 269–287.

15. This concern is discussed in, for example, Michael A. Turner, *Why Secret Intelligence Fails* (Dulles, VA: Potomac Books, 2005), and James B. Bruce and Roger Z. George, "Intelligence Analysis—The Emergence of a Discipline," in George and Bruce (2008), 1–15.

16. See Fingar, "Office of the Director of National Intelligence" (2011).

17. Analyst–customer relations are discussed in Chapter 3. See also Mark M. Lowenthal, *Intelligence: From Secret to Policy,* fourth edition (Washington, DC: CQ Press, 2009), Chapter 9; and Richard K. Betts, *Enemies of Intelligence: Knowledge and Power in American National Security* (New York: Columbia University Press, 2007), Chapter 4.

18. See Lowenthal 2009, Chapter 9; and Betts 2007, Chapter 4. See also ICD 208.

19. The Intelligence Community is normally described, accurately, as comprised of sixteen agencies (that is, the Central Intelligence Agency, the Defense Intelligence Agency, the Federal Bureau of Investigation, the National Geospatial Intelligence Agency, the National Reconnaissance Office, the National Security Agency, the Department of Justice's Drug Enforcement Administration Office of National Security Intelligence, the Department of Energy's Office of Intelligence and Counterintelligence, the Department of Homeland Security's Office of Intelligence and Analysis, the Department of State's Bureau of Intelligence and Research, the Department of the Treasury's Office of Intelligence and Analysis, and the intelligence components of the U.S. Army, U.S. Navy, U.S. Air Force, U.S. Marine Corps, and U.S. Coast Guard). I have added to this standard list three analytic components of the Office of the Director of National Intelligence, namely, the National Intelligence Council, the National Counterterrorism Center, and the National Counterintelligence Executive. For more detail on the roles and missions of these components, see An Overview of the United States Intelligence Community for the 111th Congress, 2009, at www.dni.gov/overview.pdf. For my views on the importance of reserving, enhancing, and integrating the mission-specific capabilities of the existing analytic components see, for example, Fingar, "Analysis in the US Intelligence Community" (2011).

20. Intelligence Reform and Terrorism Prevention Act of 2004, Public Law 108-458—Dec. 17, 2004, Sec 102(b) (hereafter Intelligence Reform Act) at www.dni .gov/history.htm.

21. I held the latter two positions concurrently from May 2005 through December 2008.

22. See Department of State, Office of the Historian, *Foreign Relations of the United States, 1945–50: Emergence of the Intelligence Establishment* (Washington, DC: U.S. Government Printing Office, 1996), at www.state.gov/www/about_state/history/ intel/index.html; and Michael Warner, "Legal Echoes: The National Security Act of 1947 and the Intelligence Reform and Terrorism Prevention Act of 2004," *Stanford Law & Policy Review*, 17:2 (2006), 303–318 at www.heinonline.org/HOL/Page?handle=hein .journals/stanlp17&id=1&size=2&collection=journals&index=journals/stanlp#3.

23. This point is developed in Chapter 2. See also The National Commission on Terrorist Attacks upon the United States, *The 9/11 Commission Report* (Washington, DC: U.S. Government Printing Office, 2004) (hereafter *9/11 Commission Report*); and Fingar, "Office of the Director of National Intelligence" (2011).

24. See "White House Review Summary Regarding 12/25/2009 Attempted Terrorist Attack," January 7, 2010, at www.whitehouse.gov/the-press-office/white-house-review-summary-regarding-12252009-attempted-terrorist-attack.

25. Writing these words reminds me of the oft-repeated exchanges that I had with one of the best analysts I have ever met. About every six months, for years, Chris would come to see me and decry the escalation of demands, unreasonable deadlines, too few analysts to examine all the information we received, disappointing software, and so on. He always had suggestions as well as complaints, but his main reason for coming was to unload. Every such conversation ended the same way, namely, with Chris saying, "God, I love this job. I can't believe I get paid to do something I love this much." There are few analysts as good as Chris, but many share his love of the job.

26. See, for example, Office of the Director of National Intelligence, Analytic Transformation: Unleashing the Potential of a Community of Analysts, September 2008, at http://odni.gov/content/AT_Digital%2020080923.pdf. I plan to prepare a separate book describing and explaining each of the elements in the transformation agenda, why we adopted the approach that we did with respect to each of the components, and what we learned along the way.

27. On intelligence as a profession, see Rebecca Fisher and Rob Johnston, "Is Intelligence Analysis a Discipline?" in George and Bruce (2008), 55–69.

28. Intelligence Reform Act.

29. See 9/11 Commission Report; U.S. Senate, Report of the Select Committee on Intelligence on the U.S. Intelligence Community's Prewar Intelligence Assessments on Iraq together with Additional Views, 108th Congress, 2d Session, S. Report 108-301,

July 9, 2004, at www.intelligence.senate.gov/108301pdf; and Commission on the Intelligence Capabilities of the United States Regarding Weapons of Mass Destruction, *Report to the President of the United States* (Washington, DC: U.S. Government Printing Office, 2005).

30. See "Bush Administration Implements WMD Commission Recommendations," White House News Release, June 29, 2005, at www.whitehouse.gov/news/releases/2005/06/print/20050629-2.html.

31. The formal delegation of authority is contained in *Intelligence Community Directive 200: Management, Integration, and Oversight of Intelligence Community Analysis,* January 8, 2007, at www.dni.gov/electronic_reading_room/ICD_200.pdf, but Negroponte made the delegation in 2005 using legacy Director of Central Intelligence Directives.

32. Nancy Bernkopf Tucker, "The Cultural Revolution in Intelligence: Interim Report," *The Washington Quarterly,* Spring 2008, 47–61.

Chapter 2

1. See, for example, Nicholas Florenza, "NATO to Deploy Full-Motion Video," *Aviation Week,* August 5, 2009, at www.aviationweek.aero/aw/generic/story_generic .jsp?channel=defense&id=news/DTI-VID.xml&headline=NATO%20to%20Deploy%20Full-Motion%20Video.

2. See, for example, Raymond T. Odierno, Nichoel E. Brooks, and Francesco P. Mastracchio, "ISR [Intelligence, Surveillance, and Reconnaissance] Evolution in the Iraqi Theater," *JFQ,* 50, third quarter 2008 at www.ndu.edu/inss/Press/jfq_pages/editions/i50/14.pdf; and "USAF Releases More Full Motion Video," July 20, 2009, at www.youtube.com/watch?v=wQzRACORUAc.

3. See, for example, Michael Hoffman, "More ISR Intel Analysts Needed," *Air Force Times,* August 20, 2008, at www.airforcetimes.com/news/2008/08/airforce_intel_jobs_081808/.

4. I did this in my capacity as deputy director of national intelligence for analysis, using authority delegated to me by Director of National Intelligence John Negroponte via *Intelligence Community Directive 200.*

5. For a different example of "crateology," see John Diamond, "Trained Eye Can See Right through Box of Weapons," *USA Today,* August 17, 2006, at www.usatoday .com/news/world/2006-08-17-missiles-iran_x.htm.

6. See U.S. Senate, Report of the Select Committee on Intelligence on the US Intelligence Community's Prewar Intelligence Assessments on Iraq together with Additional Views, 108th Congress, 2d Session, S. Report 108-301, July 9, 2004, 200–201, at http://intelligence.senate.gov/108301.pdf; and U.S. Senate, Report of the Select Committee on Intelligence on Postwar Findings about Iraq's WMD Programs and Links to

Terrorism and How They Compare with Prewar Assessments Together with Additional Views, 109th Congress, 2nd Session, September 8, 2006, 40–41, at http://intelligence .senate.gov/phaseiiaccuracy.pdf.

7. Brief discussions of the importance Intelligence Community use of commercial imagery can be found in Matt O'Connell, "A Leap Forward in Intelligence Gathering," *Defense Systems*, January 20, 2010, at www.defensesystems.com/Articles/2010/01/27/ Industry-Perspective-GeoEye.aspx; and Eric Rosenbach and Aki J. Peritz, "Overhead Surveillance," Belfer Center for Science and International Affairs, July 2009, at http:// belfercenter.ksg.harvard.edu/publication/19159/overhead_surveillance.html.

8. Corroboration is always a challenging and tricky activity, not least because efforts to mislead or deceive foreign intelligence services often involve planting information in ways that ensure it will be picked up by both open collectors (for example, journalists and diplomats) and clandestine collectors (such as spies). Obtaining the information in one or the other or even both channels does not necessarily make it accurate. See, for example, James B. Bruce and Michael Bennett, "Foreign Denial and Deception: Analytical Imperatives," in Roger Z. George and James B. Bruce, eds., *Analyzing Intelligence: Origins, Obstacles, and Innovations* (Washington, DC: Georgetown University Press, 2008), 122–137.

9. See, for example, European Parliament, Report on the Existence of a Global System for the Interception of Private and Commercial Communications (ECHELON Interception System) (2001/2098(INI)), July 11, 2001, at www.europarl.europa.eu/sides/ getDoc.do?pubRef=-//EP//NONSGML+REPORT+A5-2001-0264+0+DOC+PDF+V0// EN&language=EN.

10. Public and congressional debate on "warrantless wiretapping" were triggered by James Risen and Eric Lichtblau, "Bush Lets U.S. Spy on Callers without Courts," *New York Times*, December 16, 2005, at www.nytimes.com/2005/12/16/politics/16program .html. See also J. Michael McConnell, Statement, Senate Committee on the Judiciary, Hearing on the Foreign Intelligence Surveillance Act and Implementation of the Protect America Act, September 25, 2007, at www.dni.gov/testimonies/20070925_testimony .pdf.

11. See, for example, "Legal Standards for the Intelligence Community in Conducting Electronic Surveillance," February 2000, at www.fas.org/irp/nsa/standards .html.

12. See, for example, Elizabeth B. Bazan and Jennifer K. Elsea, Presidential Authority to Conduct Warrantless Electronic Surveillance to Gather Foreign Intelligence Information, Congressional Research Service, January 5, 2006, at www.fas.org/sgp/ crs/intel/m010506.pdf; and J. Michael McConnell, Statement for the Record, House Permanent Select Committee on Intelligence, Hearing on the Protect America Act of 2007, September 20, 2007, at www.dni.gov/testimonies/20070920_testimony.pdf. On

walls between intelligence and law enforcement, see the National Commission on Terrorist Attacks upon the United States, *The 9/11 Commission Report* (Washington, DC: U.S. Government Printing Office, 2004).

13. Responsibilities of the Civil Liberties Protection Officer are specified in U.S. Code, Title 50, Chapter 15, Subchapter 1, Section 403-3d. Civil Liberties Protection Officer, at www.law.cornell.edu/uscode/uscode50/usc_sec_50_00000403----003d.html.

14. See Roger Z. George and Harvey Rishikof, Editors, *The National Security Enterprise: Navigating the Labyrinth* (Washington, DC: The Georgetown University Press, 2011).

15. See, for example, "Arms: Beijing Surprise: Missiles for the Saudis," *Time*, April 11, 1988, at www.time.com/time/magazine/article/0,9171,967149,00.html.

16. Jim Woolsey has used the image many times. See, for example, his confirmation hearing for the post of director of Central Intelligence, as reported in Douglas Jehl, "C.I.A. Nominee Wary of Budget Cuts," *New York Times*, February 3, 1993, at www.nytimes.com/1993/02/03/us/cia-nominee-wary-of-budget-cuts.html?pagewanted=1.

17. Examples include Worldwide Threat Assessment Brief to the Senate Select Committee on Intelligence by the Director of Central Intelligence John M. Deutch, February 22, 1996, at www.cia.gov/news-information/speeches-testimony/1996/dci_speech_022296.html; Statement by Director of Central Intelligence George J. Tenet on the Worldwide Threat in 2000: Global Realities of Our National Security, March 21, 2000, at www.cia.gov/news-information/speeches-testimony/2000/dci_speech_032100.html; and Dennis C. Blair, director of National Intelligence, Annual Threat Assessment of the U.S. Intelligence Community for the Senate Select Committee on Intelligence, February 2, 2010, at www.dni.gov/testimonies/20100202_testimony.pdf.

18. Statement by Director of Central Intelligence George J. Tenet before the Senate Select Committee on Intelligence on the "Worldwide Threat 2001: National Security in a Changing World," February 7, 2001, at www.cia.gov/news-information/speeches-testimony/2001/UNCLASWWT_02072001.html; and Thomas Fingar, acting assistant secretary of state for intelligence and research, Statement before the Senate Select Committee on Intelligence Hearing on Current and Projected National Security Threats to the United States, February 7, 2001, at www.fas.org/irp/congress/2001_hr/s010207f.html.

19. Dennis C. Blair, director of national intelligence, Annual Threat Assessment of the U.S. Intelligence Community for the Senate Select Committee on Intelligence, February 12, 2009, at www.dni.gov/testimonies/20090212_testimony.pdf.

20. See Lucian Niemeyer, *Africa: The Holocausts of Rwanda and Sudan* (Albuquerque: University of New Mexico Press, 2006).

21. See, for example, "Summary of the White House Review of the December 25 Attempted Terrorist Attack," at www.whitehouse.gov/sites/default/files/summary_of_wh_review_12-25-09.pdf; and Eric Lipton, Eric Schmitt, and Mark Mazzetti, "Review

of Jet Bomb Plot Shows More Missed Clues," *New York Times*, January 17, 2010, at www.nytimes.com/2010/01/18/us/18intel.html?hp.

22. For additional detail, see Patrick E. Tyler, "No Chemical Arms Aboard China Ship," *New York Times*, September 6, 1993, at www.nytimes.com/1993/09/06/world/no-chemical-arms-aboard-china-ship.html; "Statement by the Ministry of Foreign Affairs of the People's Republic of China on the 'Yin He' Incident," September 4, 1993, at www.nti.org/db/china/engdocs/ynhe0993.htm; and Department of State Daily Press Briefing, September 7, 1993, at http://dosfan.lib.uic.edu/ERC/briefing/daily_briefings/1993/9309/930907db.html.

23. See DCI Statement on the Belgrade Chinese Embassy Bombing, House Permanent Select Committee on Intelligence Open Hearing, July 22, 1999, at www.cia.gov/news-information/speeches-testimony/1999/dci_speech_072299.html; and Ministry of Foreign Affairs of the People's Republic of China, "U.S.-Led NATO's Attack on the Chinese Embassy in the Federal Republic of Yugoslavia," November 15, 2000, at www.mfa.gov.cn/eng/wjb/zzjg/bmdyzs/gjlb/3432/3441/t17317.htm.

24. See J. Alexander and Azita Ranjbar, "Killing Friends, Making Enemies: The Impact and Avoidance of Civilian Casualties in Afghanistan," United States Institute of Peace, July 2008, at www.usip.org/resources/killing-friends-making-enemies-impact-and-avoidance-civilian-casualties-afghanistan; and U.N. News Center "Civilian Casualties in Afghanistan Keep Rising, Finds U.N. Report," July 31, 2009, at www.un.org/apps/news/story.asp?NewsID=31636&Cr=afghan&Cr1=civilian.

Chapter 3

1. For those too young to remember him, Rodney Dangerfield was a comedian whose tag line was, "I get no respect."

2. This is known as "Fenno's Paradox," or the belief that people generally disapprove of the U.S. Congress as a whole but approve of the member from their own district. The phenomenon has been named for the political scientist Richard Fenno, who described it in *Home Style: House Members in Their Districts* (Boston: Little, Brown, 1978). See also Stephen J. Farnsworth, "Congress and Citizen Discontent: Public Evaluations of the Membership and One's Own Representative," *American Politics Research*, 2003, 31, at http://apr.sagepub.com/cgi/reprint/31/1/66.pdf.

3. This point is developed below and in Thomas Fingar, "Analysis in the U.S. Intelligence Community: Missions, Masters, and Methods," in B. Fischoff and C. Chauvin, editors, *Intelligence Analysis: Behavioral and Social Scientific Foundations* (Washington, DC: The National Academies Press, 2011), Chapter 1.

4. The legislation that established the Office of the Director of National Intelligence (ODNI) mandated an annual report to the Congress on analytic performance. The requirement can be found in the Intelligence Reform and Terrorism Prevention Act of 2004 (hereafter Intelligence Reform Act), Public Law 108-458, December 17, 2004, at

http://frwebgate.access.gpo.gov/cgi-bin/getdoc.cgi?dbname=108_cong_public_laws&docid=f:publ458.108.pdf. The specific requirement is at Section 1019. A subset of analytic products is evaluated by the ODNI's Office of Analytic Integrity and Standards using the criteria specified in *Intelligence Community Directive 203: Analytic Standards* (hereafter ICD 203), June 21, 2007, at www.dni.gov/electronic_reading_room/ICD_203.pdf. Many more are evaluated by agency teams using the same standards, but much more could and should be done. For additional information on the importance of evaluation see National Research Council, *Intelligence Analysis for Tomorrow* (Washington, DC: The National Academies Press, 2011).

5. Flaws and lessons of the 2002 Iraq WMD estimate are discussed in Chapter 6, and in Remarks and Q and A by the Deputy Director of National Intelligence for Analysis and Chairman of the National Intelligence Council Dr. Thomas Fingar, The Council on Foreign Relations, New York, New York, March 18, 2008, at www.dni.gov/speeches_2007.htm. For other critiques of the analytic tradecraft in that estimate, see U.S. Senate, Report of the Select Committee on Intelligence on the U.S. Intelligence Community's Prewar Intelligence Assessments on Iraq Together with Additional Views, 108th Congress, 2d Session, S. Report 108-301, July 9, 2004 (hereafter SSCI 2004), at www.intelligence.senate.gov/108301pdf; and U.S. Senate, Report of the Select Committee on Intelligence on Postwar Findings about Iraq's WMD Programs and Links to Terrorism and How They Compare with Prewar Assessments Together with Additional Views, 109th Congress, 2d Session, September 8, 2006, at http://intelligence.senate.gov/phaseiiaccuracy.pdf. Deficiencies in the broader system or process for collecting, assessing, and communicating intelligence are examined in Commission on the Intelligence Capabilities of the United States Regarding Weapons of Mass Destruction, *Report to the President of the United States* (hereafter *WMD Commission Report*) (Washington, DC: U.S. Government Printing Office, 2005).

6. Mark Lowenthal has made this point more eloquently and more passionately. See, for example, Mark M. Lowenthal, "Intelligence in Transition: Analysis after September 11 and Iraq," in Roger Z. George and James B. Bruce, editors, *Analyzing Intelligence: Origins, Obstacles, and Innovations* (Washington, DC: Georgetown University Press, 2008), 226–237; and "The Real Intelligence Failure? Spineless Spies," *The Washington Post*, May 25, 2008, at www.washingtonpost.com/wp-dyn/content/article/2008/05/22/AR2008052202961.html.

7. See Remarks by Director of National Intelligence Mike McConnell, at the Conference on Strengthening Analytic Practice: Lessons from the World of Journalism, sponsored by the DNI's Office of Analytic Integrity and Standards and the Woodrow Wilson Center for Scholars, November 13, 2007 at www.dni.gov/speeches_2007.htm. See also Colin L. Powell, Opening Remarks before the Senate Government Affairs Committee, September 13, 2004, at www.fas.org/irp/congress/2004_hr/091304powell.html.

8. See ICD 203.

9. Much has been written on the need for caution in expressing confidence in analytic judgments. Intelligence analysts can learn much of value from Philip E. Tetlock, *Expert Political Judgment: How Good Is It? How Can We Know?* (Princeton, NJ: Princeton University Press, 2005). See also National Research Council, *Intelligence Analysis for Tomorrow* (Washington, DC: The National Academies Press, 2011).

10. This point is developed at greater length in Chapter 6. See also Fingar, Remarks and Q and A.

11. For elaboration see Fingar, "Analysis in the U.S. Intelligence Community."

12. Short descriptions of components of the Intelligence Community and the missions they support can be found in *An Overview of the United States Intelligence Community for the 111th Congress*, 2009, at www.dni.gov/overview.pdf.

13. For elaboration, see Fingar, "Analysis in the U.S. Intelligence Community."

14. For additional details on the incident, see Shirley Kan et al., China–U.S. Aircraft Collision Incident of April 2001: Assessments and Policy Implications, Congressional Research Service, updated October 10, 2001, at www.fas.org/sgp/crs/row/RL30946.pdf.

15. This point is developed further in Chapter 4. See also Jack Davis, "Improving CIA Analytic Performance: Strategic Warning," The Sherman Kent Center for Intelligence Analysis, Occasional Papers, 1:1 (September 2002), at www.cia.gov/library/kent-center-occasional-papers/vol1no1.htm.

16. See, for example, Jack Davis, "Improving CIA Analytical Performance: Analysts and the Policymaking Process," The Sherman Kent Center for Intelligence Analysis, Occasional Papers, 1:2 (September 2002), at www.cia.gov/library/kent-center-occasional-papers/vol1no2.htm; John McLaughlin, "Serving the National Policymaker," in George and Bruce, *Analyzing Intelligence,* 71–81; and James B. Steinberg, "The Policymaker's Perspective: Transparency and Partnership," in George and Bruce, *Analyzing Intelligence*, 82–90.

17. See, for example, Richard L. Russell, *Sharpening Strategic Intelligence* (New York: Cambridge University Press, 2007), and WMD Commission Report.

18. At the suggestion of the President's Intelligence Advisory Board, I initiated the preparation of briefing materials and oral briefings that could be used by analysts in all components of the Intelligence Community to introduce new policy-making officials to the work of the Community and how best to tap its capabilities. These briefing materials had a common core but were adjusted to suit the specific missions and operating styles of different customers. Similar materials were prepared for members of Congress by the Kennedy School's Belfer Center for Science and International Affairs. See Eric Rosenbach and Aki J. Peritz, "Confrontation or Collaboration? Congress and the Intelligence Community: Background Memos on the Intelligence Community," July 2009, at http://belfercenter.ksg.harvard.edu/publication/19201/confrontation_or_collaboration_congress_and_the_intelligence_community.html.

19. See Jack Davis, "Tensions in Analyst–Policymaker Relations: Opinions, Facts, and Evidence," The Sherman Kent Center for Intelligence Analysis, Occasional Papers, 2:2 (January 2003), at www.cia.gov/library/kent-center-occasional-papers/vol2no2.htm.

20. See Roger Z. George and Harvey Rishikof, editors, *The National Security Enterprise: Navigating the Labyrinth* (Washington, DC: The Georgetown University Press, 2011).

21. See, for example, Gregory F. Treverton, "Intelligence Analysis: Between 'Politicization' and Irrelevance," in George and Bruce, *Analyzing Intelligence*, 91–105.

22. The requirement for a report to Congress on perceived politicization can be found in Intelligence Reform Act, Sec. 1020.

23. As deputy director of national intelligence for analysis, I instructed that all IC analysts be surveyed annually to determine whether, where, on what topics, and with what consequences analysts had direct experience or had heard about instances of perceived politicization. The reports are classified.

24. See James B. Bruce, "The Missing Link: The Analyst–Collector Relationship," in George and Bruce, *Analyzing Intelligence,* 191–211.

25. Thomas Fingar, "Office of the Director of National Intelligence: Promising Start Despite Ambiguity, Ambivalence, and Animosity," in George and Rishikof, *The National Security Enterprise*, 139–155.

26. The challenges of estimative analysis are examined in Chapter 5.

Chapter 4

1. See, for example, Kenneth Lieberthal, *The U.S. Intelligence Community and Foreign Policy: Getting Analysis Right*, John L. Thornton China Center Monograph series No. 2 (September 2009), at www.brookings.edu/~/media/Files/rc/papers/2009/09_intelligence_community_lieberthal/09_intelligence_community_lieberthal.pdf. Describing his approach to intelligence to a small group of reporters soon after being confirmed, Director of National Intelligence Dennis Blair said, "Virtually every piece of analysis we see on an important issue will have not only a threat section but also an opportunity section." The quotation is from Alex Kingsbury, "Dennis Blair, Obama's Spy-in-Chief, Brings a Tactical Eye to the Job," *U.S. News and World Report*, April 8, 2009, at www.usnews.com/articles/news/national/2009/04/08/dennis-blair-obamas-spy-in-chief-brings-a-tactical-eye-to-the-job.html. The full transcript of the March 26, 2009, media roundtable is available at www.dni.gov/interviews/20090326_interview.pdf.

2. The U.S. Intelligence Community's origins antedate the Declaration of Independence and were focused on discovering British intentions toward the colonies, but the first formal intelligence organizations were established during the Revolution and focused primarily on British military plans, deployments, and capabilities. In other

words, the roots of the U.S. intelligence establishment are firmly grounded in military intelligence that traditionally has been far more concerned about threats than opportunities. The "threat-oriented" origins and raison d'être were reinforced by the lessons of Pearl Harbor and the rationale for the National Security Act of 1947 that undergirds our current intelligence establishment. That said, the roots of "opportunity analysis" also go back to the Revolutionary War era, when Benjamin Franklin and other American diplomats collected and assessed intelligence on French and other countries' attitudes toward our newly declared republic and used the resultant insight to time and target appeals for assistance. See, for example, David Hackett Fischer, *Paul Revere's Ride* (New York: Oxford University Press, 1994); and Gordon S. Wood, *The Americanization of Benjamin Franklin* (New York: Penguin, 2004).

3. Prior to the stand-up of the Office of the Director of National Intelligence in 2005, Annual Threat Assessments (then called Worldwide Threat Assessments) were presented by the director of central intelligence and, at the request of specific oversight committees, the heads of selected IC component agencies, typically the Defense Intelligence Agency, the State Department's Bureau of Intelligence and Research, and the Federal Bureau of Investigation. For representative unclassified Threat Assessments, see Dennis C. Blair, director of national intelligence, Annual Threat Assessment of the U.S. Intelligence Community for the Senate Select Committee on Intelligence, February 2, 2010, at www.dni.gov/testimonies/20100202_testimony.pdf; George J. Tenet, director of central intelligence, DCI Worldwide Threat Briefing 2002: Converging Dangers in a Post 9/11 World, March 19, 2002, at www.cia.gov/news-information/speeches-testimony/2002/dci_speech_02062002.html; and Thomas Fingar, acting assistant secretary of state for intelligence and research, Statement before the Senate Select Committee on Intelligence Hearing on Current and Projected National Security Threats to the United States, February 7, 2001, at www.fas.org/irp/congress/2001_hr/s010207f.html.

4. The process is described in *Intelligence Community Directive Number 204: Roles and Responsibilities for the National Intelligence Priorities Framework*, September 13, 2007, at www.dni.gov/electronic_reading_room/ICD_204.pdf.

5. See Fulton T. Armstrong, "Ways to Make Analysis Relevant but Not Prescriptive," Central Intelligence Agency, Center for the Study of Intelligence, *Studies in Intelligence*, 46:3 (April 14, 2007), at www.cia.gov/library/center-for-the-study-of-intelligence/csi-publications/csi-studies/studies/vol46no3/article05.html.

6. See, for example, Jack Davis, "Improving CIA Analytical Performance: Analysts and the Policymaking Process," The Sherman Kent Center for Intelligence Analysis, Occasional Papers, 1:2 (September 2002), at www.cia.gov/library/kent-center-occasional-papers/vol1no2.htm; John McLaughlin, "Serving the National Policymaker," in Roger Z. George and James B. Bruce, editors, *Analyzing Intelligence:*

Origins, Obstacles, and Innovations (Washington, DC: Georgetown University Press, 2008), 71–81; and James B. Steinberg, "The Policymaker's Perspective: Transparency and Partnership," in George and Bruce, *Analyzing Intelligence*, 82–90.

7. See, for example, Gregory F. Treverton and C. Bryan Gabbard, *Assessing the Tradecraft of Intelligence Analysts* (Santa Monica, CA: RAND Corporation, 2008), at www.rand.org/pubs/technical_reports/2008/RAND_TR293.pdf.

8. For more on strategic warning, see, for example, Jack Davis, "Improving CIA Analytic Performance: Strategic Warning," The Sherman Kent Center for Intelligence Analysis, Occasional Papers, 1:1 (September 2002); and Jack Davis, "Strategic Warning: If Surprise Is Inevitable, What Role for Analysis?" The Sherman Kent Center for Intelligence Analysis, Occasional Papers, 2:1 (January 2003), at www.cia.gov/library/kent-center-occasional-papers/vol2no1.htm.

9. See John MacGaffin, "Clandestine Human Intelligence: Spies, Counterspies, and Covert Action," in Jennifer E. Sims and Burton Gerber, editors, *Transforming U.S. Intelligence* (Washington, DC: Georgetown University Press, 2005), 79–95.

10. This requirement is contained in Public Law 102-138, the Foreign Relations Authorization Act for Fiscal Years 1992–1993 for the Department of State, and for other purposes at http://fas.org/sgp/advisory/state/pl102138.html. The specific provisions are in Section 401. It reads:

> (a) CHARTER OF THE PUBLICATION—The Department of State shall continue to publish the "Foreign Relations of the United States historical series" (hereafter in this title referred to as the "FRUS series"), which shall be a thorough, accurate, and reliable documentary record of major United States foreign policy decisions and significant United States diplomatic activity. Volumes of this publication shall include all records needed to provide a comprehensive documentation of the major foreign policy decisions and actions of the United States Government, including the facts which contributed to the formulation of policies and records providing supporting and alternative views to the policy position ultimately adopted.
>
> (b) EDITING PRINCIPLES—The editing of records for preparation of the FRUS series shall be guided by the principles of historical objectivity and accuracy. Records shall not be altered and deletions shall not be made without indicating in the published text that a deletion has been made. The published record shall omit no facts which were of major importance in reaching a decision, and nothing shall be omitted for the purpose of concealing a defect of policy.

11. National Intelligence Council, *Global Trends 2025: A Transformed World* (hereafter *Global Trends 2025*), November 2008, at www.dni.gov/nic/PDF_2025/2025_Global_Trends_Final_Report.pdf.

12. For additional information on the process, see the description of the project on the National Intelligence Council website at www.dni.gov/nic/NIC_2025_project

.html. See also the transcripts of the press briefing by Thomas Fingar and Mathew Burrows at the Ronald Reagan Building and International Trade Center, November 20, 2008, at www.dni.gov/interviews/20081120_interview.pdf; and by Mathew Burrows at the Washington Foreign Press Center, November 21, 2008, at www.dni.gov/interviews/20081121_interview.pdf.

13. National Intelligence Council, *Global Trends 2010*, November 1997. Both the report and a description of how it was prepared are available at www.dni.gov/nic/special_globaltrends2010.html. The INR study was prepared as a classified document.

14. See John C. Gannon, "Intelligence Challenges for the Next Generation," Remarks to the World Affairs Council, Washington DC, June 4, 1998, at www.fas.org/irp/cia/product/ddi_speech_060598.html.

15. National Intelligence Council, *Global Trends 2015: A Dialogue about the Future with Nongovernment Experts*, December 2000, available at www.dni.gov/nic/NIC_globaltrend2015.html.

16. National Intelligence Council, "Mapping the Global Future: Report of the National Intelligence Council's 2020 Project," December 2004, at www.dni.gov/nic/NIC_globaltrend2020.html.

17. The "Fictional Scenario: A New Caliphate" is on pages 83–92.

18. See, for example, "Remarks and Q and A by the Deputy Director of National Intelligence for Analysis and Chairman, National Intelligence Council Dr. Thomas Fingar," The Atlantic Council, Washington, DC, November 20, 2008, at www.dni.gov/speeches/20081120_speech.pdf; and Thomas Fingar, "Challenges and Choices: Drivers and Decisions That Will Shape Our Future," Merida, Spain, November 11, 2009, published in Spanish with the title "Desafios y alternativa: Factores y decisiones que determinaran nuestro futuro" in Jose Felix Tezanos, ed., *Incertidumbres, Retos y Potencialidades Del Siglo XXI: Grandes Tendencias Internacionales* (Madrid: Editorial Sistema, 2010), pp. 13–29. I have also spoken on *Global Trends 2025* in Qatar, the Republic of Korea, China, and Indonesia.

19. More on the process can be found on the National Intelligence Council website at www.dni.gov/nic/NIC_2025_project.html.

20. The European Union and the Atlantic Council have conferred with the National Intelligence Council regarding ways to undertake a similar project with a more explicitly European focus, and a number of Chinese organizations have sought my advice for projects intended to put China's "rise" into a broader global context.

21. See, for example, Michael T. Klare, "Welcome to 2025: American Preeminence Ends Fifteen Years Early," *The Nation*, October 27, 2009, at www.thenation.com/doc/20091109/klare; Alan Silverleib, "U.S. Power, Influence Will Decline in Future, Report Says," CNNPolitics.com, November 20, 2008, at http://edition.cnn.com/2008/POLITICS/11/20/global.trends.report/; Scott Shane, "Global Forecast by American Intelligence Expects Al Qaeda's Appeal to Falter," *New York Times*, November 21, 2008,

at www.nytimes.com/2008/11/21/world/21intel.html; and Alex Spillius, "U.S. Influence to Decline, NIC Intelligence Report Predicts," Telegraph.co.uk, November 20, 2008, at www.telegraph.co.uk/news/worldnews/northamerica/usa/barackobama/3492802/US-influence-to-decline-NIC-intelligence-report-predicts.html.

22. See *Global Trends 2025: A Transformed World* (Excerpts), *Energy Bulletin*, November 23, 2008, at www.energybulletin.net/node/47283; "EU Will Be Globally Weak 'Hobbled Giant' by 2025: Report," *Deutsche Welle*, November 21, 2008, at www .dw-world.de/dw/article/0,2144,3810535,00.html; and Mridul Chadha, "NIC *Global Trends 2025* Report: World to See Economic Growth at the Cost of Environment and Human Life," *Red, Green and Blue*, December 29, 2008, at http://redgreenandblue .org/2008/12/29/nic-global-trends-2025-report-world-to-see-economic-growth-at-the-cost-of-environment-and-human-life/.

23. Examples include "Global Trends 2025," *Enterprise Resilience Management Blog*, November 21, 2008, at http://enterpriseresilienceblog.typepad.com/enterprise_ resilience_man/2008/11/global-trends-2025.html; and Jacquelyn S. Porth, "World's Best Thinkers Predict Resource Scarcity in 2025," *America.gov*, November 21, 2008, available at www.america.gov/st/peacesec-english/2008/November/20081121160210sj htropo.327984.html.

24. See the discussion of *Global Trends 2025* in Christopher Layne, "The Waning of U.S. Hegemony: Myth or Reality?" *International Security*, 34:1 (Summer 2009), 147–172.

25. *Global Trends 2025*, 6–14.

26. Ibid., 28–37.

27. Ibid., 60–98.

28. Ibid., 18–26.

29. Ibid., 51–59. See also Statement for the Record of Dr. Thomas Fingar, National Intelligence Assessment on the National Security Implications of Global Climate Change to 2030, House Permanent Select Committee on Intelligence and House Select Committee on Energy Independence and Global Warming, June 28, 2008, at www .dni.gov/testimonies/20080625_testimony.pdf.

30. *Global Trends 2025*, 68–74.

31. Ibid., 63–68.

32. Ibid., 41–45.

33. See Richard A. Best Jr., "Intelligence Estimates: How Useful to Congress," Congressional Research Service, updated December 14, 2007, at www.fas.org/sgp/crs/ intel/RL33733.pdf; see especially CRS-5.

34. Al Gore, *An Inconvenient Truth: The Planetary Emergency of Global Warming and What We Can Do about It* (New York: Rodale, 2006).

35. The instruction to produce a National Intelligence Estimate was contained in Section 407 of HR 2082, Intelligence Authorization Act for Fiscal Year 2008. The bill was

passed by both Houses of Congress on February 13, 2007, but was vetoed by the president on March 8, 2008. The request for an estimate on the geopolitical effects of global climate change was not the reason for the veto. See H.R. 2082 [Report No. 110-131] at www.fas.org/irp/congress/2007_cr/hr2082.html; "H.R. 2082: Intelligence Authorization Act for Fiscal Year 2008" at www.govtrack.us/congress/bill.xpd?bill=h110-2082; "Statement of Administration Policy: H.R. 2082—Intelligence Authorization Act for Fiscal Year 2008," December 11, 2007, at www.docstoc.com/docs/5791914/HR-2082-%C2%AD-Intelligence-Authorization-Act-for-Fiscal-Year; and Best, 5.

36. Fingar, National Security Implications of Global Climate Change.

37. See "Sparks Fly at Joint Hearing on National Intelligence Assessment of Climate Change's National Security Implications," June 26, 2008, at http://newsecuritybeat.blogspot.com/2008/06/sparks-fly-at-joint-hearing-on-national.html; and John Wihbey, "Covering Climate Change as a National Security Issue," The Yale Forum on Climate Change and the Media, July 17, 2008, at www.yaleclimatemediaforum.org/2008/07/covering-climate-change-as-a-national-security-issue/.

38. Because the president had vetoed the legislation mandating production of an estimate on the geopolitical effects of global climate change, the Intelligence Community was not, strictly speaking, required to do so. This was a case in which political savvy clearly trumped legal requirements. Both Houses of Congress had asked for the study; it would have been folly on our part to disregard their instruction, especially since the president's veto message did not mention this provision.

39. See Chapter 6.

40. At the time this was written, a Google search of items on the 2007 *Estimate on Iran's Nuclear Intentions and Capabilities* identified more than 26,000 items. Representative commentaries include "'High Confidence' Games," *The Wall Street Journal*, December 5, 2007, at http://online.wsj.com/article/SB119682320187314033.html?mod+opinion_main_review_and_outlooks; John R. Bolton, "The Flaws in the Iran Report," *Washington Post*, December 6, 2007, at www.washingtonpost.com/wp-dyn/content/article/2007/12/05/AR2007120502234.html; and Justin Raimondo, "Antiwar.com's Man of the Year: Thomas Fingar. He Stopped the War Party Almost Single-Handedly" at www.antiwar.com/justin/?articleid=12088. Also see Tony Karon, "Spinning the NIE Iran Report," *Time*, December 5, 2007, at www.time.com/time/world/srticle/0,8599,1691249,00.html; and Greg Simmons, "Bush Administration Credibility Suffers after Iran NIE Report," *Fox News*, December 7, 2007, at www.foxnews.com/printer_friendlystory/0,3566,315742,00.html.

41. The declassified Key Judgments of *Iran's Nuclear Intentions and Capabilities*, November 2007, are available at www.dni.gov/press_releases/20071203_release.pdf.

42. Shortcomings and lessons of the 2002 National Intelligence Estimate entitled "Iraq's Continuing Programs for Weapons of Mass Destruction" are discussed in Chapter 6.

Chapter 5

1. Hundreds of declassified estimates can be accessed through the National Intelligence Council homepage on the Director of National Intelligence website at www
.dni.gov/nic/NIC_home.html.

2. Possibly the most notorious, and certainly the most pilloried, recent estimate is the 2002 NIE entitled "Iraq's Continuing Programs for Weapons of Mass Destruction." Shortcomings of and lessons learned from this NIE are examined at greater length in Chapter 6. The two most detailed critiques of the NIE and its tradecraft are U.S. Congress, Senate, Select Committee on Intelligence, Report on Postwar Findings About Iraq's WMD Programs and Links to Terrorism and How they Compare with Prewar Assessments (hereafter SSCI Report), September 8, 2006, at http://intelligence
.senate.gov/phaseiiaccuracy.pdf; and the Report of the Commission on the Intelligence Capabilities of the United States Regarding Weapons of Mass Destruction (hereafter WMD Commission), March 31, 2005, at http://fas.org/irp/offdocs/wmd_report.pdf. For an earlier example, see commentary on "The Military Buildup in Cuba," Special National Intelligence Estimate 85-3-62, September 19, 1962, which failed to predict the deployment of Soviet intermediate- and medium-range ballistic missiles in Cuba. Examples include "Investigation of the Preparedness Program," Interim Report on the Cuban Military Buildup by the Preparedness Investigating Subcommittee, Committee on Armed Services, U.S. Senate, 88th Congress, 1st Session (Washington 1963) (usually called the Stennis Report); Klaus Knorr, "Failures in National Intelligence Estimates: The Case of the Cuban Missiles," World Politics, 16:3 (April 1964), 455–467, at www.jstor.org/stable/2009582?seq=1; and the criticism of the NIE process in general with a specific focus on the fall of the shah's regime in Iran in U.S. Congress, House, Subcommittee on Evaluation, Permanent Select Committee on Intelligence, Iran: Evaluation of U.S. Intelligence Performance Prior to November 1978, 96th Congress, 1st Session, 1979, Committee Print. Washington, DC: US Government Printing Office, 1979. For more on IC, specifically CIA, analysis of developments in Iran prior to the fall of the shah, see Robert Jervis, Why Intelligence Fails: Lessons from the Iranian Revolution and the Iraq War (Ithaca, NY: Cornell University Press, 2010), Chapter 2.

3. See, for example, Kenneth Lieberthal, The U.S. Intelligence Community and Foreign Policy: Getting Analysis Right (Washington, DC: Brookings, 2009), 12–16; and Mark M. Lowenthal, "He Blames the Israel Lobby. But the Job Wasn't Worth It," The Washington Post, March 15, 2009, at www.washingtonpost.com/wp-dyn/content/article/2009/03/13/AR2009031302096.html.

4. One of the most reported on instances in which an executive branch official gave speeches articulating a judgment not shared by the Intelligence Community involved Undersecretary of State John Bolton's characterization of Cuba's biological warfare capabilities. See, for example, Douglas Jehl, "Released E-Mail Exchanges Reveal More Bolton Battles," New York Times, April 24, 2005, at http://query.nytimes

.com/gst/fullpage.html?res=9C03EEDD1531F937A15757C0A9639C8B63&sec=&spon
=&pagewanted=all; and Douglas Jehl, "Bolton Asserts Independence on Intelligence,"
New York Times, May 12, 2005, at http://query.nytimes.com/gst/fullpage.html?res=
9401EEDB1030F931A25756C0A9639C8B63&sec=&spon=&pagewanted=2.

5. Prior to the standup of the Office of the Director of National Intelligence in
2005, Annual Threat Assessments (then called Worldwide Threat Assessments) were
presented by the Director of Central intelligence and, at the request of specific oversight
committees, the heads of selected IC component agencies, typically the Defense Intelligence Agency, the State Department's Bureau of Intelligence and Research, and the
Federal Bureau of Investigation. For representative unclassified threat assessments, see
Dennis C. Blair, director of national intelligence, "Annual Threat Assessment of the
U.S. Intelligence Community for the Senate Select Committee on Intelligence," February 2, 2010, at www.dni.gov/testimonies/20100202_testimony.pdf; George J. Tenet,
Director of Central Intelligence, "DCI Worldwide Threat Briefing 2002: Converging
Dangers in a Post 9/11 World," March 19, 2002, at www.cia.gov/news-information/
speeches-testimony/2002/dci_speech_02062002.html; and Thomas Fingar, acting assistant secretary of state for intelligence and research, "Statement before the Senate Select Committee on Intelligence Hearing on Current and Projected National Security
Threats to the United States," February 7, 2001, at www.fas.org/irp/congress/2001_hr/
s010207f.html.

6. "McLaughlin: NIE Is Not as Decisive as It May Seem," CNN, December 10,
2007, at http://edition.cnn.com/2007/POLITICS/12/10/mclaughlin.commentary/index
.html?iref=allsearch.

7. All analysts engage in estimative analysis at least some of the time and in most
of the jobs they hold during the course of their careers, but many of them will have
little or very infrequent direct experience in the production of NIEs. The situation is
compounded by demographics; roughly half of all IC analysts have been in the Intelligence Community for less than ten years, and few have yet held positions that would
give them direct insight into the NIE process. That said, I should have been more
aware of this misunderstanding when I served as deputy director of national intelligence for analysis and done more to ensure that all analysts received information on
the points made in this essay.

8. Sherman Kent's writings on estimative analysis are more detailed and operational than are my descriptions in this essay, but any differences are matters of emphasis and intended audience and should not be interpreted as more than that. See,
for example, "Sherman Kent and the Board of National Estimates: Collected Essays,"
Central Intelligence Agency, Center for the Study of Intelligence, March 19, 2007, at
www.cia.gov/library/center-for-the-study-of-intelligence/csi-publications/books-
and-monographs/sherman-kent-and-the-board-of-national-estimates-collected-
essays/toc.html. See also Harold P. Ford, *Estimative Intelligence: The Purposes and*

Problems of National Intelligence Estimates, revised edition (Lanham, MD: University Press of America, 1993).

9. National Intelligence Council, "NIC Mission," at www.dni.gov/nic/NIC_about .html.

10. See, for example, "National Intelligence Estimates and the NIE Process," in the declassified version of the key judgments of "Prospects for Iraq's Stability: Some Security Progress but Political Reconciliation Elusive," August 2007, at www.dni.gov/ press_releases/20070823_release.pdf.

11. See, for example, Greg Miller, "Bush Goes Public with Terror Study," *Los Angeles Times*, September 27, 2006, at http://articles.latimes.com/2006/sep/27/nation/ na-terror27; and Eric Rosenbach and Aki J. Peritz, "National Intelligence Estimates," Belfer Center for Science and International Affairs, John F. Kennedy School of Government, Harvard University, July 2009, at http://belfercenter.ksg.harvard.edu/publication/ 19150/national_intelligence_estimates.html.

12. The composition of the National Intelligence Board is described in *Intelligence Community Directive 202: National Intelligence Board* (July 16, 2007). It can be found at www.dni.gov/electronic_reading_room/ICD_202.pdf.

13. Intelligence Community analysts criticized by members of Congress for the inaccuracy of IC estimates may enjoy skimming the history of cost increases and project completion dates for the Capitol Visitors' Center. For examples, see Stephen W. Stathis, "The Capitol Visitors' Center: An Overview," Congressional Research Service, updated July 22, 2003, at http://lugar.senate.gov/services/pdf_crs/The_Capitol_ Visitors_Center_An_Overview.pdf; Statement of David M. Walker, comptroller general of the United States, "Capitol Visitor Center: Current Status of Schedule and Estimated Cost," Testimony before the Subcommittee on Legislative, Committee on Appropriations, House of Representatives, July 15, 2003, at www.gao.gov/new.items/ d031014t.pdf; and statement of Terrell G. Dorn, "Capitol Visitor Center: Construction Expected to Be Completed within Current Budget Estimate," Testimony before the Subcommittee on the Legislative Branch, Committee on Appropriations, House of Representatives, July 23, 2009, at www.gao.gov/new.items/d09925t.pdf. During the period covered by these reports, the projected cost went from $351.3 million to $621 million, and the completion date slipped from December 2005 to early 2010.

14. See, for example, Robert M. Hathaway and Jordan Tama, "The U.S. Congress and North Korea during the Clinton Years: Talk Tough, Carry a Small Stick," *Asian Survey*, 44:5 (Sept.–Oct. 2004), 711–733.

15. See Richard K. Betts, *Enemies of Intelligence: Knowledge and Power in American National Security* (New York: Columbia University Press, 2007), Chapter 3.

16. The "N" appended to the name of the party stands for Nawaz Sharif, who heads the party. The PML(N) is the original and largest faction of the Pakistan Muslim League.

17. See, for example, K. Alan Kronstadt, *Pakistan–U.S. Relations*, Congressional Research Service, February 6, 2009, at www.fas.org/sgp/crs/row/RL33498.pdf.

18. The unclassified key judgments from this estimate are available at www.dni .gov/press_releases/20070202_release.pdf.

19. The unclassified key judgments from this update are available at www.dni.gov/ press_releases/20070823_release.pdf.

20. For an unclassified example of such analysis by the media, see Sara Miller Llana and Peter Ford, "Chavez, China Cooperate on Oil, but for Different Reasons," *Christian Science Monitor*, January 3, 2008, at www.csmonitor.com/World/Americas/ 2008/0103/p06s01-woam.html.

21. Available in the table reproduced in the unclassified "Key Judgments from Iran: Nuclear Intentions and Capabilities," November 2007, at www.dni.gov/press_releases/ 20071203_release.pdf.

22. Ibid.

23. A short, unclassified summary of the missile sale can be found on the NTI website at www.nti.org/e_research/profiles/saudi_arabia/missile/index.html#fnB4. See also "Arms: Beijing Surprise: Missiles for the Saudis," *Time*, April 11, 1988, at www.time.com/ time/magazine/article/0,9171,967149,00.html.

24. Congress—or individual members—requested NIEs on Iran, Afghanistan, Iraq, and climate change.

25. See Paul R. Pillar, "The Right Stuff," *The National Interest*, 91 (Sept.–Oct. 2007), 53–59.

26. See SSCI Report and WMD Commission.

27. See, for example, Michael Isikoff and Mark Hosenball, "The Flip Side of the NIE," *Newsweek*, July 18, 2007, at www.newsweek.com/id/32962.

28. See Chapter 6; and Jervis, *Why Intelligence Fails*, Chapter 3, especially 126–127.

Chapter 6

1. National Intelligence Council, Iraq's Continuing Programs for Weapons of Mass Destruction [hereafter Iraq WMD], October 2002. Declassified key judgments released on July 18, 2003, are available at www.fas.orf/irp/cia/products/iraq-wmd.html.

2. Specific deficiencies of the Iraq WMD estimate are described at great length in U.S. Senate, "Report of the Select Committee on Intelligence on the U.S. Intelligence Community's Prewar Intelligence Assessments on Iraq Together with Additional Views," 108th Congress, 2d Session, S. Report 108-301, July 9, 2004 (hereafter SSCI 2004), at www.intelligence.senate.gov/108301pdf; and U.S. Senate, "Report of the Select Committee on Intelligence on Postwar Findings about Iraq's WMD Programs and Links to Terrorism and How They Compare with Prewar Assessments Together with Additional Views," 109th Congress, 2d Session, September 8, 2006, at http://intelligence

.senate.gov/phaseiiaccuracy.pdf. Deficiencies in the broader system or process for collecting, assessing, and communicating intelligence are examined in Commission on the Intelligence Capabilities of the United States Regarding Weapons of Mass Destruction, "Report to the President of the United States" (hereafter WMD Commission Report) (Washington, DC: U.S. Government Printing Office, 2005).

3. My assessment of how the confluence of ire at the quality of intelligence and the way it was used to justify the invasion of Iraq and how the findings and political skill of the 9/11 Commission made possible and shaped the Intelligence Reform and Terrorism Prevention Act of 2004 is summarized in Thomas Fingar, "Office of the Director of National Intelligence: Promising Start Despite Ambiguity, Ambivalence, and Animosity," in Roger George and Harvey Rishikof, editors, *The National Security Enterprise: Navigating the Labyrinth* (Washington, DC: Georgetown University Press, 2011), 139–155. See also Paul R. Pillar, "Intelligence, Policy, and the War in Iraq," *Foreign Affairs*, 85:2 (Mar–Apr 2006), 15–27.

4. See, for example, SSCI 2004, Section XI, 299–300.

5. The Iraq WMD estimate was anomalous in one important respect, namely, that it was not indicative of the quality of work done by most analysts, in most agencies, on most issues, most of the time. Thousands of analysts were tarred with the sins of the relatively few, including me, who had worked on the Iraq WMD estimate. Most analytic products were not as bad as that NIE, but they were not as good as they could or should be. All are now better because the aftermath of the Iraq WMD estimate made complacency and business as usual impossible to sustain.

6. See, for example, Rep. Anna G. Eshoo, "Intelligence Needed on Climate Change," *San Francisco Examiner*, June 6, 2007, at www.annaeshoo4congress.com/anna/pdf/ AE-article-intelligence-climate-change.pdf.

7. See Richard A. Best Jr., "Intelligence Estimates: How Useful to Congress," Congressional Research Service, updated December 14, 2007, at www.fas.org/sgp/crs/intel/ RL33733.pdf.

8. See, for example, Mark Mazzetti and Eric Schmitt, "U.S. Study Is Said to Warn of Crisis in Afghanistan," *New York Times*, October 8, 2008, at www.nytimes.com/ 2008/10/09/world/asia/09afghan.html?_r=1; and Jonathan S. Landay, Warren P. Strobel, and Nancy A. Youssef, "New U.S. Intelligence Report Warns 'Victory' Not Certain in Iraq," *McClatchy Newspapers*, October 7, 2008, at www.mcclatchydc.com/world/ story/53605.html. At the time these reports were published, both of these estimates were in very preliminary form, and neither had yet attained the status of a first draft.

9. I held these positions from May 2005 through December 2008.

10. Formal delegation of authority for analytic products is spelled out in *Intelligence Community Directive 200: Management, Integration, and Oversight of Intelligence Community Analysis*, January 8, 2007. It can be found at www.dni.gov/electronic_ reading_room/ICD_200.pdf. Negroponte had, however, delegated the authority to me

in the first weeks after the standup of the Office of the Director of National Intelligence in 2005 using legacy Director of Central Intelligence directives.

11. An additional reason for anticipating intense interest in the Iran nuclear NIE was the initially small but soon growing concern, expressed to me directly by a number of members of Congress, that the president was preparing for war with Iran. An early, and largely erroneous, article both reflecting and fueling these concerns was Seymour M. Hersh, "The Iran Plans: Would President Bush Go to War to Stop Tehran from Getting the Bomb?" *The New Yorker*, April 17, 2006, at www.newyorker.com/archive/2006/04/17/060417fa_fact.

12. The National Intelligence Board (NIB) consists of the heads of all analytic components of the intelligence community and provides formal review of all National Intelligence Estimates. Meetings of the NIB are chaired by the director of national intelligence. The NIB is the successor organization to the National Foreign Intelligence Board (NFIB), which performed a similar function for the Director of Central Intelligence prior to creation of the Office of the Director of National Intelligence in 2004. The members of the NFIB that reviewed both the Iraq WMD estimate and the 2007 Iran nuclear NIE were Thomas Fingar (principal deputy assistant secretary of state for intelligence and research in 2002 and deputy director of national intelligence for analysis in 2007), Michael V. Hayden (director of the National Security Agency in 2002 and Director of the Central Intelligence Agency in 2007), James R. Clapper (director of the National Geospatial Intelligence Agency in 2002 and undersecretary of defense for intelligence in 2007), and Charles E. Allen (Assistant Director of Central Intelligence for Collection in 2002 and undersecretary of homeland security for intelligence and analysis in 2007). For additional information on the National Intelligence Board, see *Intelligence Community Directive Number 202: National Intelligence Board*, July 16, 2007, at www.dni.gov/electronic_reading_room/ICD_202.pdf.

13. The process of reform and analytic transformation did not end in 2007; it continues to this day and should continue indefinitely.

14. See, for example, Doug Bandow, "Don't Start the Second Gulf War," *National Review Online*, August 12, 2002, at www.nationalreview.com/script/printpage.p?ref=/comment/comment-bandow081202.asp. For a more exhaustive review of this period, see Louis Fisher, "Deciding on War against Iraq: Institutional Failures," *Political Science Quarterly*, 118:3 (2003), at http://loc.gov/law/help/usconlaw/pdf/PSQ-Fisher.pdf. See also Bob Woodward, *Plan of Attack* (New York: Simon and Schuster, 2004).

15. Brent Scowcroft, "Don't Attack Saddam," *Wall Street Journal*, August 15, 2002, at www.opinionjournal.com/editorial/feature.html?id=110002133. See also Todd S. Purdum and Patrick E. Tyler, "Top Republicans Break with Bush on Iraq Strategy," *New York Times*, August 16, 2002, at www.nytimes.com/2002/08/16/world/top-republicans-break-with-bush-on-iraq-strategy.html.

16. See, for example, Alison Mitchell and David E. Sanger, "Bush to Put Case for Action in Iraq to Key Lawmakers," *New York Times*, September 4, 2002. The text of the President's U.N. speech can be found at www.cbsnews.com/stories/2002/09/12/national/main521781.shtml.

17. For Byrd's remarks, see *Congressional Record*, 148: S8966 (daily edition, September 20, 2002).

18. The letters are summarized in SSCI 2004, Section XI. See also George Tenet, *At the Center of the Storm* (New York: HarperCollins, 2007), Chapter 17.

19. SSCI 2004, Section XI.

20. Ibid., Conclusion 89.

21. Tenet, 321–322.

22. Ibid.

23. SSCI 2004, Section XI, excerpt from Senator Durbin's letter.

24. See, for example, SSCI 2004.

25. Although the final report of the Joint Congressional Inquiry published in December 2002 had not yet been issued and did not phrase the matter of analyst timidity as I have, I think that the suggestion that analysts should "lean forward" more than they did and should have underscored their forward-leaning judgments in ways that would prompt decision makers to take defensive measures is implied by the exchanges summarized in that report. See Senate Select Committee on Intelligence and U.S. House Permanent Select Committee on Intelligence, "Joint Inquiry into Intelligence Community Activities before and after the Terrorist Attacks of September 11, 2001", 107th Congress, 2d Session, S. Rept. No. 107-351, H. Rept. No. 107-792, December 2002, at www.gpoaccess.gov/serialset/creports/pdf/fullreport_errata.pdf.

26. The formal name of the Rumsfeld Commission is the Commission to Assess the Ballistic Missile Threat to the United States. The commission submitted its report in July 1998; the full report is classified, but the executive summary is available at www.fas.org/irp/threat/bm-threat.htm. The Jeremiah Report, prepared by retired Admiral David E. Jeremiah, assesses the Intelligence Community's performance on the Indian nuclear tests conducted in May 1998. The report is classified, but it is described in DCI Tenet's testimony before the Senate Select Committee on Intelligence on June 2, 1998, at www.fas.org/irp/cia/product/jeremiah-decl.pdf.

27. The declassified Key Judgments can be found in Iraq WMD.

28. The importance of considering alternatives featured prominently in the Jeremiah Report, the recommendations of the WMD Commission, and the Intelligence Reform and Terrorism Prevention Act of 2004, Public Law 108-458—Dec. 17, 2004, Sec 102 (b) (hereafter Intelligence Reform Act) at www.dni.gov/history.htm. The requirement to consider alternative hypotheses was codified in *Intelligence Community Directive 203: Analytic Standards* (hereafter ICD 203), June 25, 2007, at www.dni.gov/electronic_reading_room/ICD%20203.pdf.

29. See Robert Jervis, *Why Intelligence Fails: Lessons from the Iranian Revolution and the Iraq War* (Ithaca, NY: Cornell University Press, 2010), Chapter 3; and Thomas Graham Jr. and Keith A. Hansen, *Preventing Catastrophe: The Use and Misuses of Intelligence in Efforts to Halt the Proliferation of Weapons of Mass Destruction* (Stanford, CA: Stanford University Press, 2009), Chapter 5.

30. The requirement to identify assumptions is spelled out in ICD 203.

31. Requirements for specification of and judgments regarding sources are spelled out in ICD 203 and *Intelligence Community Directive 206: Sourcing Requirements for Disseminated Analytic Products*, October 17, 2007, at www.dni.gov/electronic_reading_room/ICD%20206,%20Sourcing%20Requirements.pdf.

32. Tenet.

33. In addition to the Intelligence Community Directives cited in notes 28 and 31, see the "What We Mean When We Say: An Explanation of Estimative Language" box now included in all estimates, in the publicly released portion of the *Iran Nuclear Intentions and Capabilities* estimate at www.dni.gov/press_releases/20071203_release.pdf.

34. SSCI 2004, 298.

35. The text of the White Paper is available at www.cia.gov/library/reports/general-reports-1/iraq_wmd/Iraq_Oct_2002.htm. See also Michael Isikoff and David Corn, *Hubris: The Inside Story of Spin, Scandal, and the Selling of the Iraq War* (New York: Crown, 2006), Chapter 8.

36. SSCI 2004, 286–297.

37. The National Security Council Deputies Committee serves as the sub-Cabinet interagency forum for consideration of policy issues affecting national security.

38. See Dana Priest, "Congressional Oversight of Intelligence Criticized; Committee Members, Others Cite Lack of Attention to Reports on Iraqi Arms, Al Qaeda Threat," *The Washington Post*, April 27, 2004, A1.

39. Manu Raju, Elana Schor, and Ilan Wurman "Few Senators Read Iraq NIE Report," *The Hill*, June 19, 2007, at http://thehill.com/leading-the-news/few-senators-read-iraq-nie-report-2007-06-19.html.

40. Ibid.

41. Iraq WMD (emphasis added).

42. "Statement by David Kay on the Interim Progress Report on the Activities of the Iraq Survey Group (ISG) Before the House Permanent Select Committee on Intelligence, The House Committee on Appropriations, Subcommittee on Defense, and the Senate Select Committee on Intelligence," October 2, 2003, at www.fas.org/irp/cia/product/dkay100203.html; *Iraq Survey Group Final Report*, September 30, 2004, at www.globalsecurity.org/wmd/library/report/2004/isg-final-report/; SSCI 2004; and WMD Commission Report.

43. See, for example, the WMD Commission Report.

44. Powell's February 5, 2003, presentation at the United Nations can be found at www.globalsecurity.org/wmd/library/news/iraq/2003/iraq-030205-powell-un-17300pf.htm. See also, Tenet, Chapter 20; and SSCI 2004, Section VII.

45. See Chapter 5.

46. See Chapter 2.

47. See Nancy Bernkopf Tucker, "The Cultural Revolution in Intelligence: Interim Report," *The Washington Quarterly*, 31:2 (Spring 2008), 47–61.

48. Analysis 101 was the subject of a National Public Radio report by Mary Louise Kelley entitled, "Intelligence Community Unites for 'Analysis 101'" at www.npr.org/templates/story/story.php?storyId=10040625.

49. ICD 203 and ICD 206.

50. The reports sent to the Congress are classified. They discuss the performance of the IC as a whole and do not discuss, compare, or contrast the performance of individual agencies.

51. Two such recurring criticisms are that the Intelligence Community still cannot "connect the dots" and that it continues to squander effort on "turf battles" at the expense of undefined but presumably more important objectives. Little effort is made to explain what is meant by either criticism or to provide more than the same oft-repeated examples without context. Examples include David Goldstein, "14 Intelligence Failures Found in Christmas Day Bomb Attempt," *McClatchy Newspapers*, May 18, 2010, at www.mcclatchydc.com/2010/05/18/94417/14-intelligence-failures-found.html; David Ignatius, "Dennis Blair Erred—But He Had an Impossible Job," *The Washington Post*, May 20, 2010, at http://voices.washingtonpost.com/postpartisan/2010/05/dennis_blair_erred_—_but_he_h.html; Shane Harris, "Too Much Information," *The Wall Street Journal*, February 13, 2010, at http://online.wsj.com/article/NA_WSJ_PUB:SB10001424052748704820904575055481363319518.html; and Kasie Hunt, "Intelligence Agencies' Internal Turf Wars," *Politico*, January 20, 2010, at www.politico.com/news/stories/0110/31686.html.

52. WMD Commission Report, 6.

53. An illustrative example of ways in which I used the NIC and the PDB to pilot new ways of doing things is my instruction that Richard Immerman, my second assistant deputy for analytic integrity and standards, would attend NIE "peer review" sessions with a mandate to intervene on tradecraft issues as he deemed appropriate. Initially, he was perceived as an interloper by many of the national intelligence officers who convened these sessions, but it took only a few sessions for him to be welcome as a valuable participant whose contributions reinforced the authority of NIOs to enforce tradecraft standards. Also instructive is the fact that we had to secure the approval of IC lawyers before he could participate.

54. The PDB is both a specific product and the process through which a common core of intelligence and intelligence-derived insights are conveyed to senior members

of the national security establishment and through which they convey questions and assignments to the Intelligence Community. Although the focus here is on the product, changes to the process were also important. For additional detail, see Fingar, "Office of the Director of National Intelligence."

55. Undertakings that elicited skepticism or opposition included plans to train analysts from across the IC jointly (rather than with just other analysts from their home agency) in "Analysis 101," making far more documents available to "all" analysts through the collaborative workspace known as "A-Space," and making the existence of—but not necessarily access to—all disseminated intelligence discoverable by any analyst. On A-Space, see, for example, Larry Shaughnessy, "CIA, FBI Push 'Facebook for spies'" at www.cnn.com/2008/TECH/ptech/09/05/facebook.spies/index.html; and "Time's Best Inventions of 2008," *Time*, October 30, 2008, at www.time.com/time/specials/packages/article/0,28804,1852747_1854195_1854171,00.html. On discoverability, see *Intelligence Community Directive 501: Discovery and Dissemination or Retrieval of Information within the Intelligence Community*, January 2009, at www.dni.gov/electronic_reading_room/ICD_501.pdf.

56. Estimates can and often do play a very important pedagogic role by exposing less experienced and often more junior analysts to the thinking and expertise of colleagues who have worked a problem for years or decades. Indeed, I think this may be one of the most important functions of the NIE process because it directly and indirectly upgrades individual skills and agency capabilities on subjects that would not have been selected for NIE treatment if they were not of high and continuing importance. In the case of the Iran nuclear estimate, however, I made the conscious decision to eschew tutorial benefits in favor of demonstrated competence and ability to process large amounts of complex information very quickly.

57. See Hersh, "The Iran Plans." This was one of the earliest and most influential sources of concern about an impending attack, but, at least in my experience, such concern remained at a relatively low level until 2007.

58. See Public Law 109-364, October 17, 2006, Section 1213, at http://frwebgate.access.gpo.gov/cgi-bin/getdoc.cgi?dbname=109_cong_public_laws&docid=f:publ364.109.pdf.

59. See "Guidance on Declassification of National Intelligence Estimate Key Judgments," October 24, 2007, at www.fas.org/irp/dni/nie-declass.pdf.

60. See, for example, John Perr, "GOP in 2007: CIA 'Misleading,' and 'Anti-Bush Cabal' behind a 'Coup d'Etat,'" Crooks and Liars, at http://crooksandliars.com/jon-perr/gop-2007-cia-misleading-anti-bush-cabal.

61. See the publicly released version of the Key Judgment of "Iran: Nuclear Intentions and Capabilities," November 2007, at www.dni.gov/press_releases/20071203_release.pdf.

62. See "Statement by the Principal Deputy Director of National Intelligence Dr. Donald M. Kerr," December 3, 2007, at www.dni.gov/press_releases/20071203_statement.pdf.

63. See "Guidance on Declassification of National Intelligence Estimate Key Judgments."

64. See, for example, Mark Mazzetti, "U.S. Says Iran Ended Atomic Arms Work," *New York Times*, December 3, 2007, at www.nytimes.com/2007/12/03/world/middleeast/03cnd-iran.html?_r=1; Dafna Linzer and JobyWarrick, "U.S. Finds That Iran Halted Nuclear Arms Bid in 2003," *The Washington Post*, December 4, 2007, at www.washingtonpost.com/wp-dyn/content/article/2007/12/03/AR2007120300846.html; Mike Shuster and Melissa Block, "NIE Report on Iran Contradicts Bush Claims," *NPR*, December 3, 2007, at www.npr.org/templates/story/story.php?storyId=16846056; and Greg Miller, "Iran's Nuclear Ambitions on Hold, U.S. Agencies Conclude," *Los Angeles Times*, December 4, 2007, at www.latimes.com/news/nationworld/world/la-fg-iran4dec04,0,2695315.story?page=2.

65. "'High Confidence' Games," *The Wall Street Journal*, December 5, 2007, at http://online.wsj.com/article/SB119682320187314033.html?mod+opinion_main_review_and_outlooks.

66. John R. Bolton, "The Flaws in the Iran Report," *Washington Post*, December 6, 2007, at www.washingtonpost.com/wp-dyn/content/article/2007/12/05/AR2007120502234.html.

67. See, for example, Ray McGovern, "CIA, Iran, and the Gulf of Tonkin," Consortiumnews.com, January 12, 2008, at www.consortiumnews.com/2008/011108a.html. The most extreme example is Justin Raimondo, "Antiwar.com's Man of the Year: Thomas Fingar. He Stopped the War Party Almost Single-Handedly," at www.antiwar.com/justin/?articleid=12088.

68. For more on the ways in which the Iran nuclear NIE was characterized by various commentators and officials, see Tony Karon, "Spinning the NIE Iran Report," *Time*, December 5, 2007, at www.time.com/time/world/srticle/0,8599,1691249,00.html; and Greg Simmons, "Bush Administration Credibility Suffers after Iran NIE Report," *Fox News*, December 7, 2007, at www.foxnews.com/printer_friendlystory/0,3566,315742,00.html.

Chapter 7

1. The legislation that created the Office of the Director of National Intelligence, the Intelligence Reform and Terrorism Prevention Act of 2004 (hereafter Intelligence Reform Act) passed both houses of Congress on December 7, 2004, and was signed by President George W. Bush on December 17, 2004 (see, for example, "S.2845 Intelligence Reform and Terrorism Prevention Act of 2004" at www.govtrack.us/congress/

bill.xpd?bill=s108-2845). John D. Negroponte was nominated to serve as the first director of national intelligence on February 17, 2005; he was confirmed by the Senate on April 21, 2005 (see Scott Shane, "Negroponte Confirmed as Director of National Intelligence," *New York Times*, April 22, 2005, at www.nytimes.com/2005/04/22/politics/22intel.html?pagewanted=print&position=). Negroponte asked me to become the first deputy director of national intelligence for analysis in early May, and I accepted a few days later. See Douglas Jehl, "New Intelligence Chief Begins Rounding Out His Office's Structure," *New York Times*, May 7, 2005, at http://query.nytimes.com/gst/fullpage.html?res=9C02E4DD1530F934A35756C0A9639C8B63&sec=&spon=&pagewanted=2.

2. See The National Commission on Terrorist Attacks upon the United States, *The 9/11 Commission Report* (Washington, DC: U.S. Government Printing Office, 2004) (hereafter 9/11 Commission Report); U.S. Senate, Report of the Select Committee on Intelligence on the U.S. Intelligence Community's Prewar Intelligence Assessments on Iraq Together with Additional Views, 108th Congress, 2d Session, S. Report 108-301, July 9, 2004 (hereafter *SSCI 2004*), at www.intelligence.senate.gov/108301pdf; and Report of the Commission on the Intelligence Capabilities of the United States Regarding Weapons of Mass Destruction (hereafter WMD Commission), March 31, 2005, at http://fas.org/irp/offdocs/wmd_report.pdf.

3. For a concise history of intelligence review and reform efforts, see Michael Warner and J. Kenneth McDonald, *US Intelligence Community Reform Studies since 1947* (Washington, DC: Strategic Management Issues Office, Center for the Study of Intelligence, Central Intelligence Agency, April 2005).

4. These and other Intelligence Community Directives are available at www.dni.gov/electronic_reading_room.htm. For additional discussion of the importance of evaluation, feedback, and continuous learning, see B. Fischoff and C. Chauvin, editors, *Intelligence Analysis: Behavioral and Social Scientific Foundations* (Washington, DC: The National Academies Press, 2011); and National Research Council, *Intelligence Analysis for Tomorrow* (Washington, DC: The National Academies Press, 2011).

5. See Richards J. Heuer Jr. and Randolph H. Pherson, *Structured Analytic Techniques for Intelligence Analysis* (Washington, DC: CQ Press, 2010).

6. The term *competitive analysis* was used in the Intelligence Community's founding legislation, the National Security Act of 1947, and was retained through subsequent revisions, including the Intelligence Reform Act of 2004. The term was also used in the 1981 version of Executive Order 12333, which provides additional direction for the conduct of U.S. Intelligence Activities (text available at www.fas.org/irp/offdocs/eo12333.htm). When EO 12333 was revised in 2008, references to competitive analysis were replaced by a requirement to accurately represent appropriate alternative views and that appropriate departments and agencies of the Intelligence Community have

access to intelligence and receive the support needed to perform independent analysis (text available at http://nodis3.gsfc.nasa.gov/displayEO.cfm?id=EO_13470_). The goal, in both cases, was to ensure that USG decision makers could obtain informed "second opinions" from analysts working in different components of the Intelligence Community. Earlier versions of the law and executive order sought to guarantee this through the independence of IC components; the 2008 revisions aimed to ensure that greater integration of the IC did not result in the stifling of alternative views. On the newspaper wars of the late nineteenth and early twentieth centuries, see, for example, James McGrath Morris, *Pulitzer: A Life In Politics, Print, and Power* (New York: Harper-Collins, 2010); and David Nasaw, *The Chief: The Life of William Randolph Hearst* (New York: Martin Books, 2000).

7. The combination of adjectives is mine but see, for example, Amy B. Zegart, *Flawed by Design: The Evolution of the CIA, JCS, and NSC* (Stanford, CA: Stanford University Press, 1999).

8. See *Intelligence Community Directive 205: Analytic Outreach*, July 16, 2007, at www.dni.gov/electronic_reading_room/ICD_205.pdf.

9. Intelligence Reform Act. Integration is a central theme and goal of the two versions of the *National Intelligence Strategy* that have been issued since the establishment of the Office of the Director of National Intelligence. See *The National Intelligence Strategy of the United States of America: Transformation through Integration*, October 2005, at www.dni.gov/publications/NISOctober2005.pdf; and *The National Intelligence Strategy of the United States of America*, August 2009, at www.dni.gov/reports/2009_NIS.pdf.

10. My confirmation hearing before the Senate Committee on Foreign Relations was held on June 14, 2004. I have been unable to locate a transcript of the proceedings.

INDEX

CPSIA information can be obtained
at www.ICGtesting.com
Printed in the USA
LVHW111917080621
689705LV00008B/527